# GR

'Reading aloud is the best way to get your
children hooked on books for life'
**Jacqueline Wilson**
Children's Laureate

It's great for children to be read to every day – but it's
also great for those who get to do the reading too! A
fantastic opportunity to show off your vocal talents,
a chance to spend quiet time with your child and a
brilliantly fun way to pass an hour or just a few minutes!
We've gathered together this collection of fabulous books
through suggestions from publishers, booksellers,
librarians and children's books experts. The advice in
these pages should help you choose the most fun and
exciting books to read to your children – and they're all
ones you'll be happy to read over and over again! We have
top tips on each book from Julia Eccleshare, children's
books editor at the *Guardian*, and booksellers and
librarians have added their thoughts on why the books
are great fun to listen to. All the books should be
available in your local bookstore and are reasonably
priced. With extra recommendations from celebrities and
well-known children's authors, GREAT BOOKS TO
READ ALOUD is an invaluable tool for any family.

## Enjoy!

For more information on the books please visit:
www.greatbookstoreadaloud.co.uk

## GREAT BOOKS TO READ ALOUD

A CORGI BOOK  978 0 552 55498 5 (from January 2007)
0 552 55498 7

Published in Great Britain by Corgi Books,
an imprint of Random House Children's Books

This edition published 2006

1 3 5 7 9 10 8 6 4 2

Set in Garamond and Rockwell

Corgi Books are published by Random House Children's Books,
61–63 Uxbridge Road, London W5 5SA,
a division of The Random House Group Ltd,
in Australia by Random House Australia (Pty) Ltd,
20 Alfred Street, Milsons Point, Sydney, NSW 2061, Australia,
in New Zealand by Random House New Zealand Ltd,
18 Poland Road, Glenfield, Auckland 10, New Zealand,
and in South Africa by Random House (Pty) Ltd,
Isle of Houghton, Corner Boundary Road & Carse O'Gowrie,
Houghton 2198, South Africa

THE RANDOM HOUSE GROUP Limited Reg. No. 954009

A CIP catalogue record for this book is available from the British Library.

Printed and bound in Denmark by Nørhaven Paperback AS

OVER 70 TRIED AND TESTED

# GREAT
# BOOKS
# TO
# READ
# ALOUD

# It's never too early to start

Jacqueline Wilson
Children's Laureate
2005-2007

I love reading. I read everywhere – curled up in an armchair, slouching on the sofa, lying in the bath, half-dozing in bed. I always read on journeys. I even read walking along, though this is silly, and I shall doubtless walk slap-bang into a lamppost one day.

When my daughter, Emma, was born I fed her and changed her and rocked her ... and read to her. She was one of those fidgety babies who barely slept and wanted to be played with all the time, which was pretty exhausting. There was just one thing that kept us both thoroughly happy and contented, and that was our reading aloud sessions. I'd sit her on my lap and cuddle her close and we'd turn the pages of a big picture book together. When there was a dog we'd go 'woof, woof' and pretend to stroke him. When there was a picture of a cake we'd pretend to eat and go 'yum, yum'. It was as simple and as basic as that.

By the time she was a toddler we were onto little stories and rhymes. We had great fun reading *Where the Wild Things Are,* roaring our terrible roars and showing our terrible claws to each other. Then we got onto all those gentle little girlie books like *Milly-Molly-Mandy*, stories I'd loved when I was little, and we talked to the animals, Little Bear and Little Grey Rabbit and Frances the Badger.

I worried that our lovely reading aloud sessions might stop when Emma started to learn to read. But we carried on, because I could read her older books she couldn't yet tackle by herself. Emma loved Victorian books so we could have a

4

wonderful wallow in *Little Women* and *What Katy Did* and *A Little Princess,* and by the time she was approaching adolescence we'd read *Jane Eyre* and *Great Expectations* together.

I don't think I was that brilliant a mum. I sometimes got tetchy and I was always a rubbish cook – but I'm so pleased we read aloud. I think it's the best gift you can give your child. It's a wonderful way of bonding together and simultaneously entering the magic world of the imagination. It's the easiest way of making sure your child is hooked on books for life.

This book is packed full of helpful suggestions for reading aloud, with top tips, an annotated list of brilliant books for all ages chosen by experts, and fascinating recommendations from a galaxy of celebrities. I hope you enjoy flicking through it – and then get started on reading aloud yourself. Read to your daughter, your son, your grandchild, your niece, your nephew, your pupils, your next-door-neighbour's child . . .

Spread the word.

*Jacqueline Wilson*

xxx

Happy Reading!

# Benefits of Reading Aloud

By
Julia Eccleshare

For all readers the advantages of listening to a story are unlimited.

First and foremost, it is fun. Sharing a book is an entirely delightful thing to do. And it's easy, too. Enjoying silly sounds together, searching under flaps for missing characters, repeating the words and linking them to the pictures is a delightful experience for all from the very youngest baby onwards.

But beyond the pleasure there are also important and significant benefits.

Reading aloud has a remarkable effect on children. It enhances children's skills, interests and development in many ways that reach far beyond just improving their own reading interests and abilities.

Listening to stories has a strong influence on personal and social growth as it gives children the chance to experience things beyond their own world and to think about other people and their lives. Hearing stories also gives children access to new words, phrases and sounds, all of which improve their spoken and written vocabulary. Sharing a story by reading it aloud can make difficult or scary things seem safer.

All of these and more are the unexpected extras that can be gained from reading aloud.

Try it!

# Ten top benefits

1  Reading aloud creates the perfect bond between parent and baby – it's cosy, comforting and it's fun.

2  Listening to stories provides children with new 'friends' – characters whom they learn to love.

3  Hearing new words gives children a richer vocabulary.

4  Children can understand stories that are beyond their own reading ability.

5  Hearing books read aloud improves a child's ability to listen for periods of time and increases attention spans.

6  Reading aloud allows children to interact by interrupting and asking questions about meaning.

7  Hearing a story read aloud enables children to make connections with others' personal experiences.

8  Listening to more complex stories can help children to extend their knowledge and understanding.

9  Listening to a story being read aloud shows beginner readers how fluent readers read.

10  The words children hear in books give them a rich language when they begin their own writing.

# It's never too young to start

☑ Don't leave it too late! Reading a story is the easiest way to 'talk' to a baby before they have any language of their own. It's never too young to start reading aloud with your child.

☑ Snuggling up together is part of the magic of reading aloud. But don't forget! Being physically close is important even when a child gets older.

☑ Sharing a book together provides the opportunity for taking off into new worlds using the vocabulary that goes with them. Take time to explain new words and to link the words and pictures.

☑ Reading aloud needs to be fun for the reader and the listener. Allow children to make their own choices as well as guiding them towards books you think they'll enjoy.

☑ Try to make time for reading every day so that it becomes part of a daily habit. Soon, it becomes something everyone can look forward to with pleasure.

☑ Build up a collection of books that you enjoy and feel free to return to them time after time. For the very young, look for books with lots of repetition and rhyme. These are easy to read with enthusiasm and children love being able to join in with the refrains. Don't worry if you have to re-read a book again and again. Repetition and familiarity are part of the pleasure for the young listener.

☑ Remember children love to revisit stories they enjoyed when they were younger. Let them read aloud their favourites to you for a change.

☑ Reading aloud doesn't need to take long. A little and often is enough to give children a head start when it comes to enjoying books on their own.

☑ Above all, make sure reading aloud is fun!

Go out and enjoy.

**SHEILA
HANCOCK**

Children's literature is so entertaining nowadays that I suspect I get even more pleasure reading to my grandchildren than they do listening to me. Their most frequent request is David McKee's *Not Now, Bernard*, because I cannot get through this tale of a monster eating a little boy and taking his place, unnoticed by his busy parents, without becoming speechless with laughter. Shared giggles are such a joy. And sharing is what reading stories is all about. When they are young, my grandchildren are subjected to my histrionic dramatization of all the tales. As they get older they read to me, and, I am glad to say, show extraordinary versatility of characterization, with Jack having a particularly fine repertoire of wolves. We have the most enormous fun.

My favourite book to read aloud is *Each Peach Pear Plum* by Janet and Allan Ahlberg. What a gem of a book. It's absolutely perfect for sharing with babies, toddlers and older children. By using fairy-story characters and nursery rhymes, the characters are immediately recognisable – and if they're not initially, they soon become so. And like the very best picture books, it holds a visual surprise on each page, culminating in a very happy finale that involves all the characters in the book having a fun feast. This is a book that, as a parent, I didn't mind reading and re-reading with my daughter. In fact, I loved coming back to it. That's what makes it so special.

**MALORIE
BLACKMAN**

**MICHAEL PALIN**

I used every opportunity I could to read to my children. My motives were invariably selfish. Reading time meant time off from fighting, shouting, arguing and making a mess. And that was just me.

All my children enjoyed being told a story. A certain calm descended as their almost limitless physical energy was projected onto the characters they were hearing about. For an actor like me, reading aloud offered a valuable chance to try out voices and characters and ham it up to a captive audience. Though, I must say, Tom, Will and Rachel always dealt sternly with any over-acting.

If the book you were reading was halfway decent there would always be cries for at least one encore.

STORY AND PICTURES BY MAURICE SENDAK

'One more page, please!'

'No, it's time for bed now.'

This always brought forth a vigorous protest from a child whose eyes had been half-closed for at least fifteen minutes.

'I'm not sleepy!'

My favourite was Maurice Sendak's brilliantly drawn fantasy *Where the Wild Things Are*. It was a tricky one because the illustrations were dense but the text economic. At one point comes the line 'Let the wild rumpus start!' followed by a fantastically lively illustration of the boy and the creatures capering madly about. Over this I would make up my own gallery of sound effects, a combination of drum-beats, chants and cries, building to the sort of aural collage that the BBC Stereophonic Workshop used to be famous for.

The sharing of the wild rumpus will always be one of the happiest memories of our time together.

© John Swannell

**CHERIE BOOTH QC**

One of the great joys of being a parent is the opportunity it gives you to read aloud with your kids. There is nothing better than to snuggle down at the end of the day with a good story to share. I don't have a particular favourite – different books suit different moods. I enjoy poems and rhyming stories that help children understand the tricks you can play with words. Other times I just love to read a book with great pictures that you can talk about. And there is nothing better than to allow your imagination to soar with a quick-moving adventure with a climax at the end of every chapter and the anticipation that tomorrow there will be more excitement.

Enjoy this sample extract from one of the most popular picture books ever! This extract gives a real taste of the rhythm and humour in *The Gruffalo*. Try it out with your child today!

# THE GRUFFALO

**The Gruffalo**
by Julia Donaldson
and Axel Scheffler
Macmillan
Children's Books

A mouse took a stroll through the
  deep dark wood.

A fox saw the mouse and the mouse
  looked good.

"*Where are you going to, little brown mouse?*
*Come and have lunch in my underground*
  *house.*"

"It's terribly kind of you, Fox,
  but no —

I'm going to have lunch
  with a gruffalo."

"*A gruffalo? What's a gruffalo?*"
"A gruffalo! Why, didn't you know?

## THE GRUFFALO

**Winner of the
Smarties
Book Prize
Gold Award**

"He has terrible tusks,

and terrible claws,

And terrible teeth in his terrible jaws."

*"Where are you meeting him?"*

"Here, by these rocks,
  And his favourite food is roasted fox."
*"Roasted fox! I'm off!"* Fox said.
*"Goodbye, little mouse,"* and away he sped.

"Silly old Fox! Doesn't he know,
  There's no such thing as a gruffalo?"

**Dear Zoo**

Rod Campbell

Campbell Books

**What is the perfect pet?**

**Why not lift the flaps and see what the Zoo has sent?**

'A book that children can really interact with.'

*Lesley Hall*
*Ottakar's Bromley*

# Dear Zoo

## Rod Campbell

The first pet is an elephant but he is too heavy. A giraffe is too tall, a lion is too fierce and a camel is too grumpy. A snake is too scary, a monkey is too naughty and a frog is too jumpy.

All of them have to go back to the Zoo.

Maybe there is no perfect pet?

But then, at the Zoo they think very hard and send . . . a puppy!

A little puppy with a lovely pink tongue and a waggy little tail.

The perfect pet!

Why share
Dear Zoo?

☑
An flap to lift
on every page
reveals a
wonderful
surprise

☑
Children love
the expectation
as they lift
each flap

☑
Total
satisfaction
when the
right pet
arrives

## Pants

Giles Andreae and
Nick Sharratt

Picture Corgi

Pants. Whatever the
size, colour or shape,
they delight children
of all ages. In just a
few bubbly words,
different kinds of
pants are celebrated
and applauded with
exuberance.

'It's hard to
suppress a giggle
when you're
reading out a story
that says "pants"
thirty-three times!'

*Emma Swabey*
*Ottakar's Science Museum*

Small pants, big pants

Giant frilly pig pants

New pants, blue pants,
one, two, three

Rich pants, poor pants

Swinging on the
door pants

How many more pants
can you see?

Giant frilly pig pants

Why share
Pants?

☑
Easy to read,
shout or sing
aloud with
everyone
joining in

☑
Lots of
repetition
makes it easy
for beginner
readers

☑
Brightly
coloured
illustrations
make all the
pants different
and fun

## We're Going on a Bear Hunt

Michael Rosen
Illustrated by
Helen Oxenbury
**Walker Books**

Fantastic adventure as a family cheerfully sets out on a brave hunt to find the bear. It could be frightening but they're not scared. They're full of confidence and excitement.

'You'll be chanting it for the rest of the day.'

*Matthew Cayton*
*Ottakar's Greenwich*

*We're going on a bear hunt,*
*We're going to catch a big one.*
*What a beautiful day!*
*We're not scared.*

**Caves, mud, rivers, forest ...
whatever obstacles the family
encounters, they resolutely
overcome them, happily
repeating the chorus:**

*We can't go over it,*

*We can't go under it,*

*Oh no! We've got
to go through it.*

**And so they do,
accompanied by
glorious noises to
describe their actions:**

*Swishy Swashy!*

*Splash Splosh!*

*Squelch Squerch!*

*Hoo Wooooo!*

**But when they find the
bear . . . they can't hurtle
home fast enough, repeating
all the noises as they go.**

Why share
We're Going on
a Bear Hunt?

☑
A fabulous
family
adventure

☑
Repetition of the
chorus on every
page means
children can
easily join in

☑
Use of words
that sound
like what they
mean, which
makes it easy
to add special
effects

# 0-5 years

## One Snowy Night

Nick Butterworth

HarperCollins Children's Books

Outside, it's snowing but Percy the Park Keeper is snug inside his hut. He makes himself a nice mug of hot cocoa and gets himself ready for bed.

But outside, the animals are not nearly as cosy. It is bitterly cold in the Park and there is not enough shelter. First the squirrel, then the rabbits, the fox, the badger, two ducks, a hedgehog and a whole family of mice come knocking on his door. They all want a bed for the night!

'A great story to get children involved by pretending they are a rabbit or a mouse or a fox . . . The big picture at the end encourages group participation.'

*Angie Crawford
Ottakar's Edinburgh*

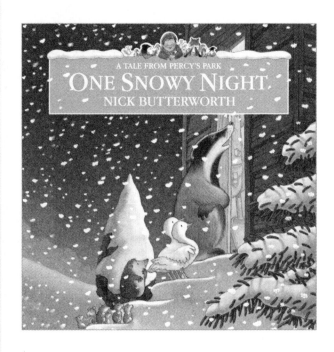

How Percy finds room for all his friends so that everyone ends up having a good night's sleep makes a perfect bedtime story.

Beautiful illustrations capture the magical world of Percy and his animal friends who live in the park.

Why share
One Snowy
Night?

☑
Percy and his
friends bring
the magic of
the animal
world to life

☑
A story
showing the
happiness that
sharing brings

☑
A celebration
of the cosiness
of bed

## Rosie's Walk

Pat Hutchins

Red Fox

Rosie the hen sets off for a walk around the farmyard. Head held high, she goes "across the yard, around the pond, over the haycock, past the mill, through the fence, under the beehives" and gets safely back home in time for her dinner.

'A classic tale of farmyard peril.'

*Vicki de'Silva*
*Ottakar's Bromley*

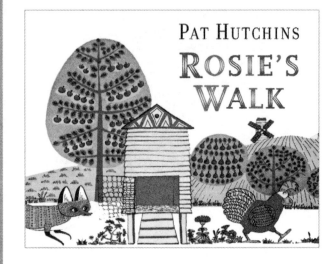

PAT HUTCHINS
ROSIE'S
WALK

But, what else is happening while Rosie goes for her walk?

Just behind the hen comes the fox. Luckily, Rosie doesn't

24

notice him and, more luckily still, things don't go so well for the fox.

Following the adventures of both the hen and the fox is thrilling – and hilarious!

Why share Rosie's Walk?

☑ Wonderful humour

☑ A multi-layered but simple story

☑ Encourages children to read pictures as well as words, and to predict outcomes.

# 0-5
## years

## The Lighthouse Keeper's Rescue

Ronda and
David Armitage

**Scholastic**

**Mr Grinling is a
lighthouse keeper
through and through.
He always has been
and it's all he wants
to be. But there's a
problem. Mr Grinling
just can't seem to
stay awake.**

When the lighthouse doesn't
light up at the right time,
the lighthouse
inspectors are
very angry. They give
Mr Grinling one last
chance . . . All goes
well until one nice
warm sunny
afternoon when Mr
Grinling falls asleep
on his way to the

But Mr Grinling and Hamish found the coastguard first. The crunching noise as the dinghy hit the launch woke Mr Grinling. For a moment he was very frightened.

lighthouse. Poor Mr Grinling! The inspectors say he can't be a lighthouse keeper any more!

But, when Mr Grinling does something very brave and special, the lighthouse inspectors come up with a clever plan. Mr Grinling can still be a lighthouse keeper but he'll have someone to help him so he can enjoy his naps too!

## The Tiger Who Came to Tea

Judith Kerr

**HarperCollins
Children's Books**

It's not every day that
you open the door to a
big, furry, stripy tiger
who says, "Excuse me,
but I'm very hungry.
Do you think I could
have tea with you?"

But that's just what
happens to Sophie and
her mummy one day.
And what an adventure
it begins!

'For anyone who has
ever had an
imaginary
friend . . . or
a real tiger!'

*Emma Swabey
Ottakar's
Science
Museum*

The hungry tiger
eats all the
sandwiches and
then all the cake.
He drinks all the
tea in the pot.
And he still
wants more. He
eats all the food
in the cupboard
and all the food
in the fridge.

Why share
The Tiger Who
Came to Tea?

☑
A magical story
about the
importance
of believing

☑
Heart-warming
illustrations
capture the
wonder of
the story

☑
A classic which
has been loved
by children for
over thirty
years

He drinks all the milk and then all the water from the taps. "Thank you for my nice tea," he says. And he's gone.

There's nothing left for supper – so Sophie and Mummy and Daddy go out to a café. They also make sure to stock up on food for the tiger in case he ever comes to tea again.

## No Matter What

Debi Gliori

**Bloomsbury**

Does love ever wear out? That's the all-important question that Small needs to have answered when he is feeling grim and grumpy and unloved.

Luckily Large knows just how to comfort Small. "Grumpy or not, I'll always love you no matter what," Large says, scooping Small up in a tight hug.

Small thinks of all the things he could be that would be unloveable, like a bear, a bug, or even a crocodile. But Large knows that no matter what, Small is loved for ever.

A warm-hearted story, illustrated with glorious pictures of Small and Large and their loving relationship, this book is made for sharing again and again.

'This endearing story requires lots of participation from listeners. Perfect to read to children or adults!'

*Grainne Cooney
Ottakar's Inverness*

## Hairy Maclary from Donaldson's Dairy

By Lynley Dodd

Puffin

**Take a handful of dogs and just one cat and what do you get? Trouble!**

**The loveable Hairy Maclary sets out for a walk from his home at Donaldson's Dairy. With his tail up and his eyes shining he steps out proudly.**

'I like to read this in the style of a horse-racing commentator . . . Children can't believe I can read it so fast!'

*Lesley Sim*
*Librarian, West Sussex*

Everywhere he goes, he is followed. Soon Hairy Maclary's friends are all stepping out behind him – including Bottomley Potts covered in spots, Hercules Morse as big as a horse, Muffin McLay like a bundle of hay, Bitzer Maloney all skinny and bony, and Schnitzel von Krumm with a very low tum. How brave the dogs look until . . . suddenly, out from the bushes, steps Scarface Claw, the toughest tom in town.

One "EEEEEOWWWFFTZ!" from Scarface and the dogs are nothing more than a scatter of paws and a clatter of claws as they hurry home to the safety of their beds.

Why share Hairy Maclary from Donaldson's Dairy?

☑ Rhyming story with lots of repetition

☑ Fast-paced story about some scaredy-cat dogs!

☑ Everyone loves Hairy Maclary!

## Is It Bedtime Wibbly Pig?

Mick Inkpen

Hodder

There are many ways of putting off bedtime – and Wibbly Pig seems to know most of them! He's happy to sit in the bath and enjoy the foam bubbles, then there's drying to be done, brushing teeth, drawing a picture in the mirror, looking at the moon and collecting up all the soft toys.

'A perfect bedtime story.'

*Emma Swabey
Ottakar's Science Museum*

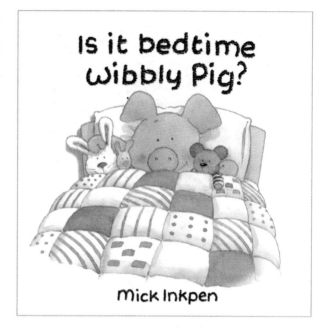

And all of it takes a lot of time which means that bedtime gets put off for longer and longer. After all, even though it's bedtime, Wibbly Pig is not tired. In fact, he's BOUNCY and going to sleep is the last thing on his mind.

Why share
Is It Bedtime
Wibbly Pig?

☑
The perfect
book for
anyone who has
battles over
bedtime!

☑
Wibbly Pig is
an adorable
character who
has many
adventures
you can enjoy

Luckily, Wibbly
Pig isn't always
right about
what he feels!

Gorgeous
illustrations
capture all of
Wibbly Pig's
tricks – and
the bliss of
sleep when
it comes.

**0-5**
years

## The Owl Who Was Afraid of the Dark

Jill Tomlinson

Illustrated by
Paul Howard

Egmont

Plop is a normal little owl baby in every way except that he's frightened of the dark. He thinks that the dark is nasty. Plop's parents send him off to find out what other people think of dark. Plop finds out that dark is when fireworks happen – which is why it's exciting and that it's when an old lady can forget that she's old – that's why it's kind.

And dark is when Father Christmas comes and fills up stockings, which makes it necessary as, without it, Father Christmas wouldn't come visiting. For the man with the telescope, dark is wonderful as it's only in the dark that the stars can be seen properly.

They can't all be wrong, can they?

How Plop learns to love the dark is a beautifully reassuring story for all.

## Where the Wild Things Are

Maurice Sendak

**Red Fox**

When Max puts on his wolf suit and makes mischief, his mother calls him 'WILD THING' and sends him to bed without any supper.

**WHERE THE WILD THINGS ARE**

**STORY AND PICTURES BY MAURICE SENDAK**

'What a wild rumpus of a book.'

*Emma Swabey*
*Ottakar's Science Museum*

Alone in his room, Max enters a magical world and sets sail across the sea to the place where the wild things are.

The wild things roar their terrible roars and gnash their terrible teeth and roll their terrible eyes and show their terrible claws . . .

But Max is not scared. Instead, Max tames the wild things and is made their king.

When things have gone far enough, Max sends the wild things off to bed without their supper and returns to the safety of his bedroom.

'This classic magical picture book will keep your child enthralled night after night after night.'

*Sam Harrison*
*Waterstone's*

## Handa's Surprise

Eileen Browne

Walker Books

Handa's got a surprise for her friend Akeyo. She's taking her a huge basket of delicious-looking fruit. She has a soft yellow banana, a sweet-smelling guava, a round juicy orange, a ripe red mango, a spiky-leafed pineapple, a creamy green avocado and a tangy passion fruit.

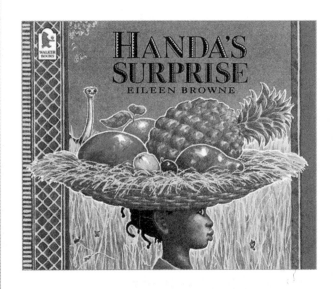

Which will Akeyo like best, wonders Handa.

But the surprise is on Handa, as she doesn't notice that there are others who are enjoying her gift as she makes her hot walk to her friend's house.

Luckily for Handa, all is not lost. Akeyo loves the fruit that Handa brings – and the animals are happy too!

She will be surprised, thought Handa
as she set off for Akeyo's village.

The simplest of stories,
perfectly and uniquely told
in words and pictures
conjuring up the delicious
fruit, the hot countryside
and the children's fun.

Why share
Handa's
Surprise?

☑
A hugely
effective joke
in which even
the very
youngest
listener is
included

☑
The very young
can 'read' the
pictures, which
tell their own
story

☑
Wonderful
illustrations
open up a
whole new
world

'Ideal to read to a
class or at home.'

*Kate Chorley*
*Ottakar's Bromley*

### Olivia

Ian Falconer

Simon and Schuster

Olivia is an endearing piglet with a lot of attitude! She's good at lots of things . . . She's very good at singing – loudly! She's very good at wearing people out. Luckily, she often wears herself out too... She likes getting dressed – which usually means trying on everything in her cupboard.

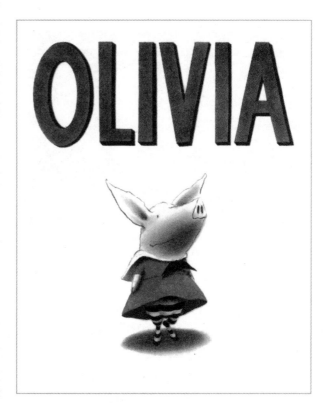

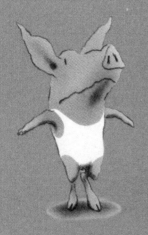

She likes to go to the beach and she likes to build sandcastles – very big sandcastles. There are some things Olivia doesn't like. Especially . . . having a nap! And she's not too keen on modern art either – and nor is Olivia's mum when she finds Olivia has tried

But there is one painting Olivia just doesn't get.
"I could do that in about five minutes," she says to her mother.

to copy it onto her bedroom wall! Join Olivia in whatever she's doing – and have fun!

Fantastic illustrations show just how endearing – and exhausting – Olivia can be!

## Not Now, Bernard

David McKee

**Red Fox**

'Hello, Dad,'
said Bernard.
'Not now, Bernard,'
said his father.

'Hello, Mum,'
said Bernard.
'Not now, Bernard,'
said his mother.'

Bernard's parents always seem to be too busy to notice him. So, when he tells them that there is a monster in the garden and it is going to eat him up, they don't come rushing out to help him . . .

'Making up voices for all the characters makes this all the more fun.'

*Jonathon Lloyd*
*Ottakar's Greenwich*

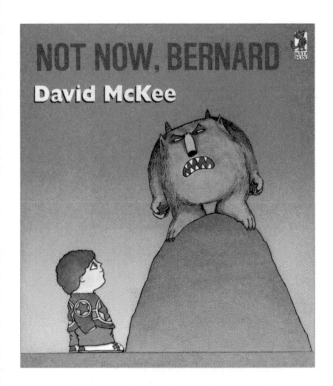

Now there's a monster in the house, and Bernard's parents still ignore him. They treat the monster as if he were Bernard, letting him read Bernard's  comics and play with his toys, giving him his supper in front of the TV and switching off his light when he's safely in bed.

"ROAR," went the monster behind Bernard's mother.

Why share
Not Now,
Bernard?

☑
An unsentimental
look at parent/
child
relationships

☑
A scary
message, but
one that makes
children feel
strong

☑
Brilliant
illustrations
reinforce the
message

A wickedly black fantasy that takes a hard look at what might happen when children are ignored. Initially scary, once children see the joke, they love it.

## The Gruffalo

Julia Donaldson and
Axel Scheffler

**Macmillan**

"A mouse took a stroll
through the deep dark
wood.

A fox saw the mouse
and the mouse looked
good."

'A present-day and
future classic, this
story should be
read to every child.'

*Emma Swabey*
*Ottakar's Science Museum*

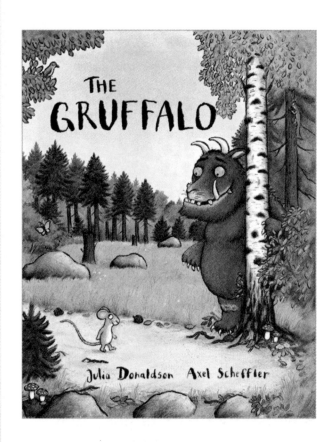

How can such a tasty little
mouse make his way safely
through the deep dark wood?
By inventing the gruffalo, a
fearsome creature with terrible
claws, terrible tusks and
terrible teeth in his terrible
jaws. He sounds so fierce and
frightening that everyone is
scared stiff of him.

The quick-thinking little mouse is soon the most powerful creature in the deep dark wood as he tricks first the fox, then the owl and then the snake into running away to hide instead.

When a gruffalo does finally appear, the little mouse scares him, too, by showing him how frightened all the animals are of him.

Clever mouse!

Why share The Gruffalo?

☑ A brilliant rhyming picture book about trickery and cunning

☑ Fabulous illustrations create the charming gruffalo

☑ A wonderful story for everyone to join in

# 0-5
## years

## Bear Snores On

Karma Wilson and
Jane Chapman

**Simon and Schuster**

Deep in his dark lair
right at the back of the
cave, Bear sleeps
through the long cold
winter. He sleeps
through the day and he
sleeps through the night
and all the time he
snores and snores and
snores . . .

'Snoring sound
effects and
joining-in are a
must with this
snuggly tale.'

*Vicki de'Silva*
*Ottakar's Bromley*

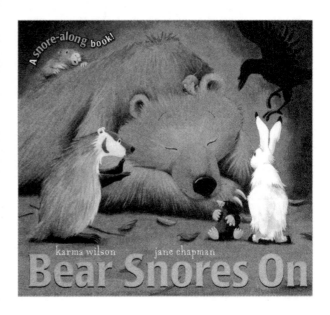

Then, an itty-bitty mouse comes
in for some shelter. It's safe and
dry in the cave, and the mouse
lights a cosy fire, but Bear
snores on . . . A hare hops in and
there's tea to share but Bear
snores on . . . A badger comes
by with a nice sack of honey-
nuts. The animals chew and
chomp and crunch but Bear
snores on . . . All the little
animals gather in the cave and
are making a delicious stew
when Bear finally wakes up.

The cold winds howl and the night sounds growl. But the bear snores on.

SNORE!

Poor Bear! He's missed all the fun but the little animals brew him fresh tea and Bear tells his story until the sun rises.

Cuddled in a heap, with his eyes shut tight, he sleeps through the day, he sleeps through the night.

☑
Lovely story
with building
momentum

☑
Warm
evocation of
what animals
do in the winter

☑
Press-button
snore means
Bear really
does snore
on and on . . .

## Owl Babies

Martin Waddell

Illustrated by
Patrick Benson

Walker Books

Everyone who's ever
missed their mummy
will love *Owl Babies*.

"Where's Mummy?"
asks Bill, the littlest
owl baby, when the
three babies wake up
in the dark, dark night
and find their mummy
has gone . . .

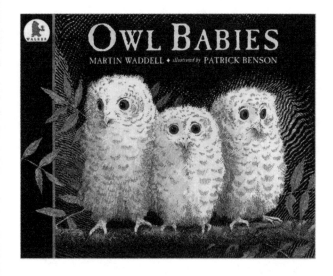

And where has she gone, the
three little babies wonder as
they cuddle up close for comfort
on a branch of the tree deep in
the heart of the forest.

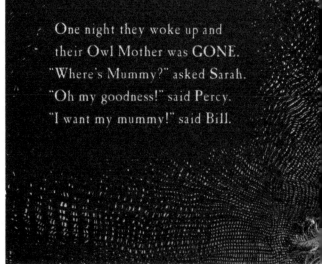

One night they woke up and
their Owl Mother was GONE.
"Where's Mummy?" asked Sarah.
"Oh my goodness!" said Percy.
"I want my mummy!" said Bill.

They think hopefully of the juicy mice she might bring, but even more than food they just want their mummy to come home to keep them safe.

Together, they close their eyes and WISH!

With a swoop of her wide wings, Mummy returns.

All is well once more!

Patrick Benson's charming illustrations delicately capture the fear and longing of the little owl babies.

# 0-5
## years

## Pumpkin Soup

Helen Cooper

**Picture Corgi**

Cat, Squirrel and Duck are three friends who do everything together, including making the most delicious pumpkin soup. Each has a specific job to do: the Cat slices up the juicy pumpkin, the Squirrel stirs in the water while the Duck carefully scoops up a pipkin of salt and tips in just enough. Everything is perfection in their lives.

'A really cosy book for bedtime with wonderful warm autumnal tones . . . A real treat.'

*Gillian Macdonald*
*Ottakar's, Edinburgh*

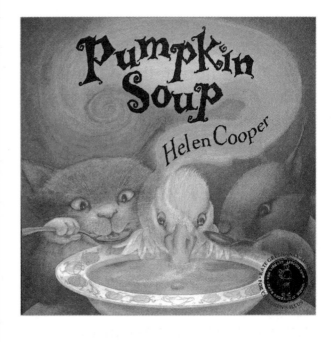

Until . . . the Duck decides that it is his turn to stir the soup. From the moment that the Duck picks up the Squirrel's spoon everything goes badly wrong and, in the row that follows, the Duck runs away. How the Cat and the Squirrel fear for his life and how far and wide they search to bring him home! At last, the Duck returns . . . and the Cat and the Squirrel let him make the pumpkin soup.

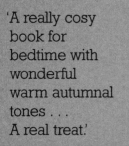

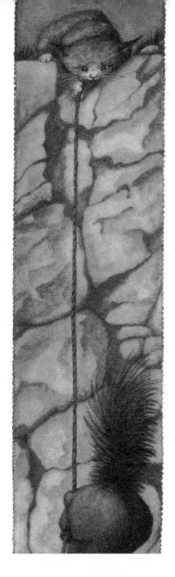

Why share
Pumpkin Soup?

☑
Warm-hearted
story about the
value of
friendship

☑
Glorious
illustrations
can be pored
over for hours

☑
Passionate
affirmation that
even the
youngest can
be useful

Helen Cooper's
exquisite illustrations
are the perfect
accompaniment to
this simply written
story about friendship
and sharing.

## Winnie the Witch

Korky Paul and
Valerie Thomas

Oxford

Winnie the Witch has a
problem. Everything in
her house is black. The
carpets are black, the
chairs are black, the bed
is black with black
sheets, the pictures on
the walls are black and
there is even a black
bath. Winnie likes it
that way.

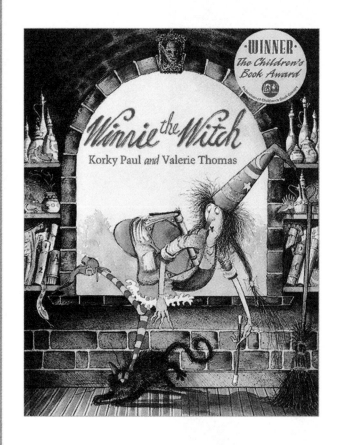

'Full of visual
detail, this book
will brighten
everyone's day.'

*Grace Print*
*Ottakar's Bromley*

But Wilbur the cat is also black and, when he closes his eyes, Winnie can't see him against all the other blacks in the house. After she's stepped on him just once too often, Winnie decides that a little magic will do the trick. ABRACADABRA! and Wilbur has a red head, a yellow body, a pink tail, blue whiskers and four purple paws. Poor Wilbur! Even the birds laugh at him when he tries to hide up in a tree. Luckily, Winnie thinks of a new trick that can put everything right!

Why share Winnie the Witch?

☑ Winnie the scatterbrained witch is a lot of fun

☑ Magical chaos is very entertaining

☑ Children will love Winnie's brightly coloured world

## The Elephant and the Bad Baby

Elfrida Vipont and Raymond Briggs

**Puffin**

When the elephant meets the Bad Baby he asks, 'Would you like a ride?' And the Bad Baby says, 'Yes.' The elephant picks up the baby with his trunk and puts him on his back and so begins a spree of madness as, off they go, rumpeta, rumpeta, rumpeta through the town, doing one bad thing after another.

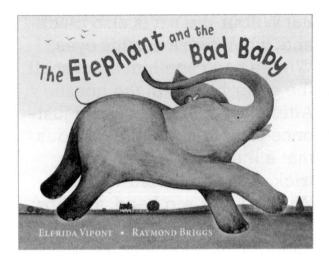

Every time the elephant asks the baby if he wants something, the baby just says 'Yes' and the elephant helps him to an ice-cream, a bun, some crisps, a lollipop and more. But the Bad Baby never once says please.

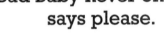

Soon, the elephant and the Bad Baby are chased through the town by all the angry shopkeepers but then the Bad Baby remembers he is only a baby and says, 'PLEASE! I want to go home to my mummy!' All is forgiven and the whole procession goes off for a feast of pancakes made by the Bad Baby's mummy.

## Angry Arthur

Hiawyn Oram and
Satoshi Kitamura

**Red Fox**

When Arthur's mum
says that he can't stay
up to watch his
favourite TV show he
gets angry. Very angry.
So angry that his anger
becomes a stormcloud
exploding thunder
and lightning and
hailstones. So angry
that it becomes a
hurricane hurling
rooftops and
chimneys
and church
spires.

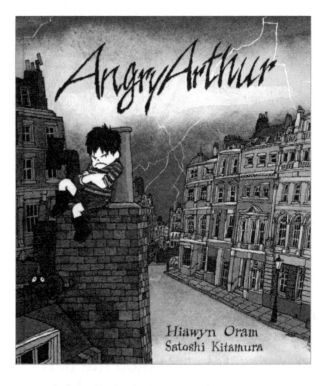

Soon Arthur finds himself
hurtling through space on an
explosion of destruction. All that
remains is Arthur and his bed.
But why is he so angry? Arthur
can't remember. Can you?

A fabulous story with incredibly vivid illustrations that capture the explosive feelings of anger and the destruction that they cause. A satisfying resolution which shows however angry you feel, you can get over it.

'A magical cautionary tale that should tantalise any tantrum-prone tyke.'

*Sam Harrison*
*Waterstone's*

## All Join In
Quentin Blake
Red Fox

A wonderful celebration of joint activities and noise! Lots of it!

" When Sandra plays
  the trumpet
  it makes a lovely
  sound

And Mervyn on his
  drum-kit
  can be heard for
  miles around

Stephanie is brilliant,
  when she plays
  the violin

But the very best of
  all is when
  we ALL JOIN IN"

'Demands everyone joins in as it invites listeners to make plenty of noise.'

*Angie Crawford*
*Ottakar's Edinburgh*

Quentin Blake's bubbly text encourages huge and cheerful sounds. Banging and clanging in 'Sorting Out the Kitchen Pans,'

some very loud QUACK QUACK QUACKs in 'Nice Weather for Ducks,' and some fantastic WHEEE!s down banisters, an elephant's trunk and on an overloaded toboggan.

But there's some nice quiet too for another kind of ALL JOIN IN – when it's time to tidy up.

Why share
All Join In?

☑
Swinging rhythms with loud choruses to share

☑
Makes life seem fun, especially when doing things together

☑
Brilliant pictures perfectly match the words

# 0-5
## years

### There Was An Old Lady Who Swallowed a Fly

Pam Adams

Child's Play

Have you ever wondered exactly what happened inside the old lady's tummy after she swallowed that fly?

In the case of this HUGE old lady, it's easy to see. There's a neat little hole right into her insides which gets bigger and bigger the more she swallows.

'Repetitive and culminative nature of the rhyme begs for it to be read aloud.'

*Jemma Cook*
*Ottakar's Clapham*

The little fly looks harmless enough but imagine what happens when it's followed by a spider, a bird, a cat, a dog, a cow – and even a horse! The cheerful old lady swallows each one to chase the others out but, needless to say, all does not go according to plan!

A wonderfully visual version of a much-loved joining-in rhyme which celebrates the ridiculous in a light-hearted way.

Why share
There Was An
Old Lady Who
Swallowed a
Fly?

☑
Repetition
makes it easy
for all to join in

☑
Die-cut hole
makes the
crowded
insides easy
to see and
encourages
participation

She swallowed the cat to catch the bird. How absurd to swallow a bird. She swallowed the bird to catch the spider, to catch the fly. She swallowed the spider that wriggled and jiggled and tickled inside her. She swallowed the fly why?

## Dig Dig Digging

Margaret Mayo
Illustrated by
Alex Ayliffe

Orchard Books

The perfect book for any machine-mad child. Diggers, tractors, fire engines, cranes, car transporters, bulldozers, dumper trucks, rubbish trucks and more. Everything you've ever wanted to know about big machines is vividly described in cheerful rhymes which celebrate the sounds of the machines.

'Try singing the story to your little ones, it won't be long before they are joining in.'

*Angie Crawford*
*Ottakar's Edinburgh*

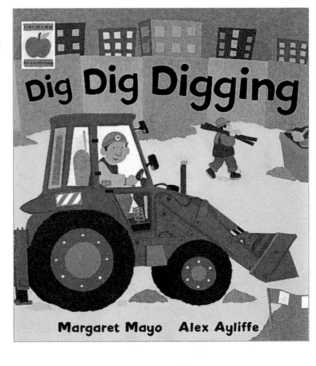

"Diggers are good at
dig, dig, digging.
Scooping up the earth
and lifting and tipping.
They make huge holes with
their dig, dig, digging;
They can work all day."

Why share
Dig Dig
Digging?

☑
Introduction to
a host of big
machines and
the jobs they do

☑
Bright pictures
display the way
machines work

Glorious double-page
spreads capture the scale
of the different vehicles
and the places that they
work. And it all ends with
a soothing night-time
scene of the machines
at rest. Perfect for bedtime!

## Doing the Animal Bop

Jan Ormerod and
Lindsey Gardiner

**Oxford**

**"If you like to dance and you sometimes sing, why don't you do the animal thing?" An irresistible invitation to join in the great animal bop. Any kind of dancing will do.**

'A simply super story that gets children walking and talking like the animals.'

*Gillian Macdonald*
*Ottakar's Edinburgh*

You can jive and jiggle and jump and wiggle with the monkeys or do the flim-flam flutter to the ostrich flounce.

You can grunt and groan and roar and rage and stomp, stomp, stomp in the rhino romp. Or you can cluck like a chicken or dance like a duck. Whatever way you like to dance and sing, the animal bop is just your thing.

Roar and rage, it's a **rhino romp!**

Why share
Doing the
Animal Bop?

☑
Great catchy
joining-in
rhymes

☑
A delightful
celebration of
having fun

☑
Words that
dance off
the page

Hopping, bopping, thumping and stomping – all the animals join in the animal bop and all readers can join in the catchy refrains too. Follow the lead of the animals through the lovely illustrations of their noisy fun!

### That's Not My Puppy...

Fiona Watt

Illustrated by
Rachel Wells

**Usborne**

How can you tell one puppy from another? By feel – in this attractive and colourful touchy-feely board book for the very young. Run your fingers over the page and every puppy feels deliciously different. Stroke them and it's easy to discover that one has a tail that is too fluffy while another has paws that are too bumpy.

'Curious young fingers will have hours of fun exploring the textures.'

*Sam Harrison*
*Waterstone's*

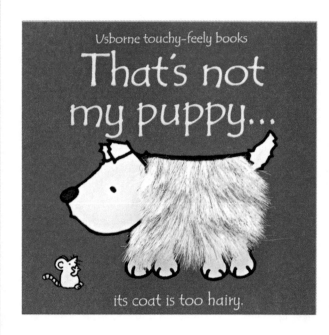

Usborne touchy-feely books

**That's not my puppy...**

its coat is too hairy.

There's one with ears that are too shaggy and one that has a very shiny collar. No two puppies are the same. But where's my puppy?

Its collar is too shiny.

Why share
That's Not My
Puppy . . .?

☑
Perfect for the
very young
to touch the
feely bits

☑
A fun book to
share as an
introduction
to different
sensations

Enjoy all the loveable puppies in words and pictures.

At last! Here it is! It's the one with the lovely squashy nose!

**ANNE FINE**

When my girls were young we spent hours idling about in our nighties in the double bed, ploughing through books from the library. They'd lie, one on each side of me, sucking their thumbs and jabbing me in the ribs with their elbows if I stopped doing the voices properly. They were some of the happiest times we had.

Then came the dark, dark years when my girls wanted to read by themselves. Now I'm thanking my lucky stars I have grandchildren and have started again at the beginning. Here's me and Isaac with our much-loved book of nursery rhymes. (You don't have to know the tunes. You just have to be bold enough to make one up and sing it with perfect confidence.) Since Isaac is currently enchanted by the notion of 'Man as Egg', one of his favourites is 'Humpty Dumpty.' But we warble them all with the greatest enthusiasm.

**RUTH KELLY MP**

I love reading to my children and they have all enjoyed *The Gruffalo* by Julia Donaldson and Axel Scheffler. A wonderfully illustrated books, it tells the story of a brave little mouse who goes on a long journey through the deep dark wood. It is a tale of ingenuity, courage and self-belief, which sparks the imagination. With both rhythm and pace, the story can be retold hundreds of times.

**J. K. ROWLING**

One of my fondest memories of my eldest daughter at age five involved *The Voyage of the Dawn Treader* by C.S. Lewis. I used to balance the book on top of a very tall standard lamp to prevent her reading on before the next bedtime. One day, while I was safely in the kitchen, she clambered up a set of shelves to reach the book, gulped down the next two chapters and then, hearing my footsteps, hastily returned it to its perch on top of the lamp. I only rumbled her because she showed absolutely no surprise when, during that night's reading, Eustace, the hero, turned into a dragon.

My two younger children are still immersed in picture books, although my son's most recent favourite is *Dr. Seuss's Green Eggs and*

**CHARLIE HIGSON**

I'm a terrible ham when it comes to reading to my kids. I like to do all the voices so I look for books with lots of dialogue and different characters. My kids are totally unimpressed, and probably prefer having my wife read to them. She reads in a very soothing voice, and she's not trying to act or show off. It reminds me of listening to my own mother read when I was a kid. In the end it doesn't really matter what you read to kids, they appreciate anything, and just like having someone there with them. I've been reading a book called *Britannia*, about English history, to my seven-year-old. He doesn't understand a word of it, but insists on having it every night. That said, it makes a huge difference if you can find a book that you can all enjoy together. My favourite is probably *Professor Branestawm*. This is a series of short stories about a mad inventor who creates ridiculous machines. It's great to be able to read something that genuinely makes your kids laugh.

**TERRY WOGAN**

Reading aloud to children is an absolute pleasure. When I was a child, one of my favourite books was *Doctor Dolittle* and I thoroughly enjoyed reading it aloud to my children when they were young. Reading aloud to children of all ages is so important as they then begin to realize that reading books themselves will give them great pleasure.

*Ham,* which, quite apart from increasing his vocabulary, can also be used to persuade him to eat omelettes. I think we own the complete works of Sandra Boynton, which are so witty and well-written; my personal favourite is *Hippos Go Berserk*, but my husband and I both know *The Going to Bed Book* off by heart and have often recited it in the dark to soothe a fractious toddler. The *Hairy Maclary* and *Slinky Malinki* books by Lynley Dodd are some of the most satisfying books to read aloud, with their rhymes building into funny stories. Finally, *The Snail and the Whale* and *The Gruffalo*, both by Julia Donaldson and illustrated by Axel Scheffler, have given literally hours of pleasure to the whole family.

**ELEANOR UPDALE**

As a small child I had the immeasurable benefit of a mother who read to us at bedtime, and there are some books I revisit with her long-lost voice echoing in my head. And what fun to read out to my own children Jill Murphy's *Peace at Last* and *A Piece of Cake* with all their humane jokes for parents hidden in the children's stories. Later we shared adventure books, *Just William*, and countless poems. We all remember them, years on. It seems that reading aloud, for the reader and the listener, engages memory in a special way, making the books more lasting treasures.

Shortly before my mother-in-law died, we recorded her reading *The Wind in the Willows* to our children. It's a rousing rendition, in her

**IMOGEN STUBBS**

We have a nine-year-old son, Jesse, who is dyslexic and until recently was no more connected to books than a mole is to the sky. And then we read *Horrid Henry's Underpants* by Francesca Simon to him. And he loved it. He immediately latched on to the characters and found them very funny. And then miracle of miracles he decided he wanted to read the stories so that he could 'play' the characters Perfect Peter, Miss Battle-Axe, Rude Ralph, Dizzy Dave, and best of all Henry himself. He now has read all the *Horrid Henries* and has them proudly in a special book rack by his bed. And now he wants

**MICHAEL MORPURGO**

When I was very young (a very long time ago but I was young once, I promise you) my mother used to read me 'The Elephant's Child' by Rudyard Kipling. She used to read me lots of poems by Edward Lear and John Masefield and Walter de la Mare, among others. But of all the poems and stories she read to me 'The Elephant's Child' was always my favourite.

I loved it partly, I'm sure, because she read it beautifully. She was an actor, but she didn't act it. She felt it. She read it as if she had made up the story herself, as if she loved it. She delighted in reading it to

deep Scottish voice, suitably menacing in all the right places. It's hard not to laugh, though, when her eyesight lets her down and 'Mr Badger' becomes 'McBadger' for a while. And it's good to know that in time my grandchildren will be able to hear her voice wrapped up in a story.

to read them with us all over again. It is starting to feel like Evelyn Waugh's *A Handful of Dust* when Tony nearly dies in the jungle and is rescued by the mad recluse, Mr Todd, who has lived in the jungle for nearly sixty years. Tony recovers but is forced to become Mr Todd's 'companion', spending the rest of his life reading aloud the works of Dickens to him. Maybe we should read that one with Jesse next!

me, I know she did. When I read the first few words of this story now all these years later, it's her voice I hear in my head. 'In the high and far-off times the Elephant, O best beloved, had no trunk.' And the story goes on to tell us how he acquired one, painfully, courtesy of a crocodile which he encounters by 'the great grey green greasy Limpopo river.' This is still my favourite story, and these days I read it aloud, to my grandchildren perhaps, or just to myself, and remember.

# Revolting Rhymes

## Little Red Riding Hood and the Wolf

**Enjoy this sample poem from Roald Dahl's *Revolting Rhymes*. A hilarious take on the classic tale, this has great pace and loads of opportunity for funny voices!**

As soon as Wolf began to feel

That he would like a decent meal,

He went and knocked on Grandma's door.

When Grandma opened it, she saw

The sharp white teeth, the horrid grin,

And Wolfie said, 'May I come in?'

Poor Grandmamma was terrified,

'He's going to eat me up!' she cried.

And she was absolutely right.

He ate her up in one big bite.

But Grandmamma was small and tough,

And Wolfie wailed, 'That's not enough!

'I haven't yet begun to feel

'That I have had a decent meal!'

He ran around the kitchen yelping,

'I've got to have a second helping!'

Then added with a frightful leer,

'I'm therefore going to wait right here

'Till Little Miss Red Riding Hood

'Comes home from walking in the wood.'

He quickly put on Grandma's clothes,

(Of course he hadn't eaten those.)

He dressed himself
in coat and hat.

He put on shoes and
after that

He even brushed
and curled his hair,

Then sat himself in
Grandma's chair.

In came the little girl
in red.

She stopped. She stared. And then she said,

'What great big ears you have, Grandma.'

'All the better to hear you with," the Wolf
replied.

'What great big eyes you have, Grandma,'
said Little Red Riding Hood.

'All the better to see you with,' the Wolf
replied.

He sat there watching her and smiled.

He thought, I'm going to eat this child.

**Revolting
Rhymes**
Roald Dahl
Illustrated by
Quentin Blake
Puffin

'Pure pleasure.
Raucous,
irreverent,
inventive.'

*Times Literary
Supplement*

Revolting Rhymes

Compared with her old Grandmamma
She's going to taste like caviare.
Then Little Red Riding Hood said, 'But
    Grandma, What a lovely great big
      furry coat you have on.'
      'That's wrong!' cried Wolf.
      'Have you forgot
      'To tell me what BIG TEETH
    I've got?
   'Ah well, no matter what you say,
'I'm going to eat you anyway.'
The small girl smiles. One eyelid flickers.
She whips a pistol from her knickers.
She aims it at the creature's head
And bang bang bang, she shoots him dead.
A few weeks later in the wood,
I came across Miss Riding Hood.
But what a change!  No cloak of red,
No silly hood
  upon her head.
She said, 'Hello, and
  do please note
'My lovely furry
  WOLFSKIN
  COAT.'

## Cosmo and the Magic Sneeze

Gwyneth Rees

**Macmillan Children's Books**

Cosmo has always wanted to be a witch-cat, just like his father, so when he passes the special test he's really excited. He can't wait to use his magic sneeze to help Sybil the witch mix her spells.

Sybil is very scary, with her green belly button and toenails, and no one trusts her. But when she starts brewing a secret spell recipe – and advertising for kittens – Cosmo and his friend Scarlett begin to worry. Could Sybil be cooking up a truly terrifying spell? And could the extra-special ingredient be **KITTENS**?

## Why share Cosmo and the Magic Sneeze?

☑ **A funny, thrilling and deliciously magical story**

☑ **Packed full of characterful illustrations**

## Horrid Henry's Big Bad Book

Francesca Simon

Illustrated by
Tony Ross

Orion

If there's something unpleasant that can be done, you can be sure that Horrid Henry will do it. In the ten hilarious stories in this collection, Horrid Henry is up to no good. He frightens the daylights out of the new teacher, he causes chaos on a school trip and he nearly drowns everyone in the swimming pool. He also has a full-scale battle with the demon dinner lady. Horrid Henry is endlessly inventive when it comes to causing trouble. And, whatever else he's doing, Henry always makes sure he can be as horrid as possible to his little brother, Perfect Peter.

FRANCESCA SIMON
HORRID
HENRY'S
BiG
BAD
BooK

*Ten favourite stories – and more!*

Illustrated by Tony Ross

## Why share
Horrid Henry's Big Bad Book?

☑ **The awfulness of Horrid Henry's behaviour provides endless entertainment**

☑ **Funny stories about everyday life – with a difference!**

☑ **Witty illustrations show just how bad Horrid Henry can be**

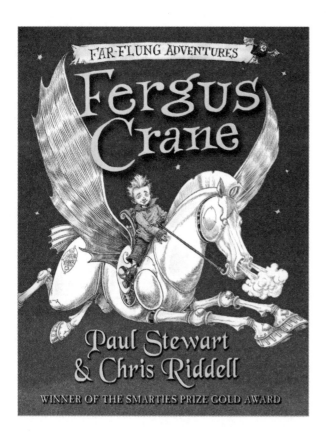

**Fergus Crane**

Paul Stewart and
Chris Riddell

Corgi Yearling

When young Fergus Crane receives three mysterious letters from his long-lost Uncle Theo, everything in his life changes. Each is delivered at midnight by a flying box and they set Fergus off on a thrilling adventure. He must leave behind his home and his mother and set off for the Emerald Sea in an attempt to save his schoolfriends from a dastardly villain. It's an exciting story as the courageous young Fergus, helped by some powerful magic which includes a winged horse who flies Fergus to Fire Island, is set against Captain Claw and his desperate pirate band. Can Fergus save the day and will he return safely to his comfortable home above Beiderbecker's Bakery?

Why share Fergus Crane?

☑ **Fergus Crane is a wonderful hero**

☑ **A warm-hearted adventure with thrills and spills of every kind**

☑ **Fantastic illustrations which add extra value to the story**

## 5-8 years

### The Sheep-Pig
Dick King-Smith
**Puffin**

A pig herding sheep? It's a preposterous idea but it is exactly what Babe does. Born the runt of the litter, the little piglet is adopted by Fly the sheep dog and brought up with her puppies. Soon Fly is training Babe in all the ways of herding sheep. But Babe proves to be even better with the sheep than his adopted mother. In fact, he's a genius at it. His secret? Babe treats the sheep with courtesy and respect. He's such a polite little chap that the sheep listen to him and do exactly as he asks. And after he's saved them from a gang of sheep-rustlers, they'll do anything for him.

A farmyard story with a difference, *The Sheep-Pig* is an exciting and unexpected adventure.

'An entertaining tale that produces a good basis for discussion afterwards.'

*Angie Crawford*
*Ottakar's Edinburgh*

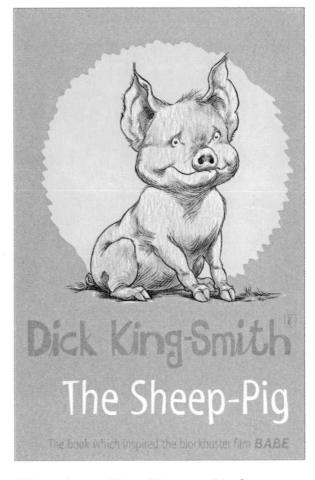

Dick King-Smith
The Sheep-Pig
The book which inspired the blockbuster film *BABE*

Why share The Sheep-Pig?

☑ **A funny and touching farmyard adventure**

☑ **Babe, the sheep-herding pig, is a brilliant and original creation**

☑ **An exhilarating story of unusual success**

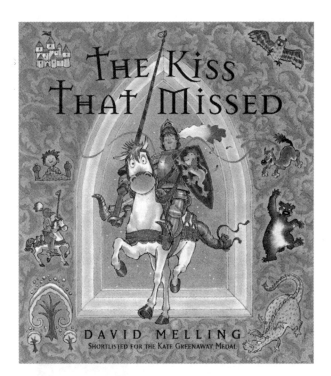

## Why share The Kiss That Missed?

☑ **Charming bedtime story with a lovely sleepy theme**

☑ **Knights and dragons and kings and castles make a perfect modern fairy story**

'The king's kiss may have missed its mark but this book certainly doesn't.'

*Nicola Cowling, Librarian, Devon*

### The Kiss That Missed
David Melling
**Hodder**

In a hurry as usual, the king blows his son a beautiful bedtime kiss. But it misses! Disaster! The kiss floats out of the castle and into the wild wood, and a poor knight is sent out to find it and bring it back. The wild wood is a dark and forbidding place where nothing good ever happens. The knight has to face bears with long claws and growly roars, swooping owls, and a pack of hungry wolves with dribbly mouths. It's scary but, luckily the kiss itself floats along in the nick of time and all the animals are lulled gently to sleep by its power. Safe at last, the knight and his horse settle down for a lovely sleep themselves – but on a rather unpredictable seat . . .

How the knight takes the kiss home makes a perfect bedtime story.

## The Iron Man
Ted Hughes
**Faber**

Taller than a house and with a head the size of a bedroom, the Iron Man appears at the top of the cliff at the beginning of one of the greatest modern fairy stories. Where he comes from, nobody knows. How he was made, nobody knows. He topples over the cliff and breaks into many pieces. It looks like the end for the Iron Man but he puts himself back together and begins a reign of terror throughout the countryside as he smashes up the farmers' tractors and diggers.

How the farmers try to bring down the Iron Man and how his powers end up being used to save the world unfolds in this brilliant and mysterious story.

'An endearing story of friendship and hope that children enjoy listening to over and over.'

*Holly de'Silva*
*Ottakar's Bromley*

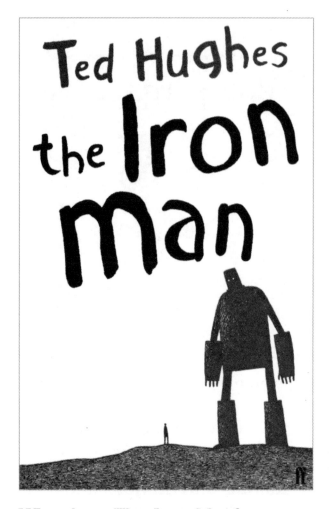

Why share The Iron Man?

☑ **Fabulous modern fable raising questions about good and evil**

☑ **A mysterious story that introduces a brilliantly imaginative creation**

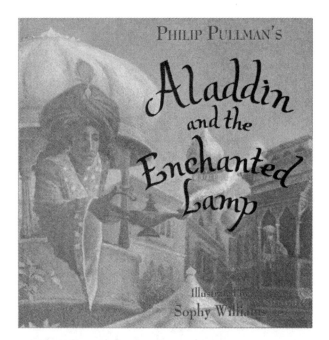

PHILIP PULLMAN'S

*Aladdin and the Enchanted Lamp*

Illustrated by
Sophy Williams

Why share Aladdin and the Enchanted Lamp?

☑ **Brilliant retelling of a classic**

☑ **Magical use of language**

☑ **Richly coloured illustrations create a fairy tale world**

**5-8**
years

**Aladdin and the Enchanted Lamp**
Philip Pullman
Illustrated by
Sophy Williams
Scholastic

'New lamps for old! New lamps for old!' is the familiar refrain of the classic story of Aladdin. And there's much, much more to it in Philip Pullman's glorious retelling which creates a world of magic, mystery, mayhem and – finally – happiness.

When Aladdin's 'uncle' turns up out of the blue, his whole life changes in a flash – literally. Shut up underground for three days, Aladdin finds himself in a wonderful cavern full of precious jewels including a magical ring and, of course, a magic lamp.

How Aladdin's and his mother's lives are changed by their new-found riches and what Aladdin learns along the way makes for a magnificent adventure.

Lots of jokes pay tribute to Aladdin's hugely popular pantomime traditions and there are lavish embellishments to the familiar story.

## Mrs Pepperpot Stories

Alf Prøysen

**Red Fox**

An old woman who sometimes shrinks to the size of a pepperpot is certainly unusual. But that's exactly what happens to Mrs Pepperpot. For no rhyme or reason she may suddenly become a tiny version of her usual self.

Being only four inches tall has a lot of disadvantages and poses many sudden dangers but, luckily, Mrs Pepperpot has plenty of magic tricks which can help her out. With a mixture of criticism and flattery, Mrs Pepperpot makes the sun shine hotly to dry her clothes, the pancakes do their own tossing in the pan and the cat give her a ride through the snow drifts which would otherwise be right over her head.

Full of hilarious surprises, the forty stories about Mrs Pepperpot are charming and wholly original.

Why share Mrs Pepperpot Stories?

☑ **A complete adventure in each short story**

☑ **A new look on life from a very small perspective**

'Will be enjoyed by listeners today as much as when they were first published.'

*Holly de'Silva, Ottakar's Bromley*

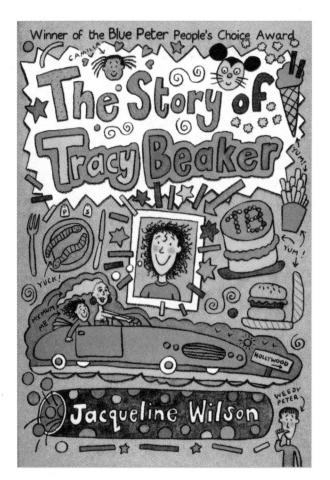

## Why share
## The Story of Tracy Beaker?

☑ **Tracy Beaker is a very special heroine**

☑ **The ups and downs of Tracy's life are funny and sad and ring very true**

### The Story of Tracy Beaker

Jacqueline Wilson
Illustrated by
Nick Sharratt

Corgi Yearling

Tracy Beaker is ten years old and she lives in a children's home. What she wants is to live in a real home with a real family but that doesn't look likely to work out. It's not that people haven't tried – there were Aunty Peggy and Uncle Sid and then there were Julie and Ted. Somehow Tracy always ends up back in the children's home. Of course, one day her glamorous mother will come and take her away but, in the meantime, Tracy has to muddle along. When a visitor comes to the home, Tracy makes a new friend. Could Cam be the foster mother Tracy has been looking for?

Tracy tells her own story in a moving but entertaining way which is also very funny.

## The Tales of Olga da Polga

Michael Bond

**Oxford**

Olga da Polga is a very special guinea pig – and she knows it! From her very grand name onwards, everything about Olga da Polga is just a little bit better than everyone else, and the stories she tells – even if they are not completely true – confirm it. Olga da Polga finds herself in a wonderful new home. All goes well until she overhears a conversation about her new name. Not being one to let matters be decided without her, Olga da Polga writes her name clearly in the sawdust for all to see. Clever Olga da Polga! More wonderful adventures about a little guinea pig with a very large imagination follow, as Olga da Polga makes a new friend, wins a prize and goes off on her travels.

'Some of the best-loved children's stories ever written.'

*Sam Harrison*
*Waterstone's*

### Why share
### The Tales of Olga da Polga?

☑ **Humorous adventures within the secret world of guinea pigs and their friends**

☑ **Olga da Polga is an original and feisty character**

## 5-8 years

### Snow White and the Seven Aliens

Laurence Anholt

Illustrated by
Arthur Robins

**Orchard Books**

Snow White has ambitions to be a seriously cool pop star. She can sing, she can dance and she can even write her own songs. But with the Mean Queen, lead singer in the Wonderful Wicked Witches, as her step-mother, Snow White knows she hasn't got a chance. Even the Mean Queen can't help noticing that Snow White is turning into a great beauty and when her weak-willed mirror finally admits it, Snow White is sent packing to a city destination which is designed to finish off her hopes for ever. Luckily, the seven singing aliens are on hand to provide all the support Snow White needs to make it big in the city!

## Why share Snow White and the Seven Aliens?

☑ **A seriously silly story that makes reading fun**

☑ **An old favourite is given a brilliant new look**

## 5-8 years

### The Pony-Mad Princess: Princess Ellie to the Rescue

Diana Kimpton

**Usborne**

Princess Aurelia is meant to spend all her time practising to be a princess. She has to learn how to smile and how to sit quietly in her pink palace bedroom. But Aurelia doesn't want to be a princess. All she wants is to be Ellie and to spend all her time in the stables with her beloved ponies. When a new groom arrives at the palace, it looks as if Ellie will have her chance. Ellie is truly happy taking care of Sundance and riding out with the other ponies. But someone is watching. Can Ellie find out who and can she rescue her beloved Sundance when disaster strikes? Ellie's courage shows just what a great princess she is.

'Fun and easy to read.'

*Sam Harrison*
*Waterstone's*

## Why share The Pony-Mad Princess?

☑ **A perfect story for all those who are pony-mad**

☑ **An exciting adventure**

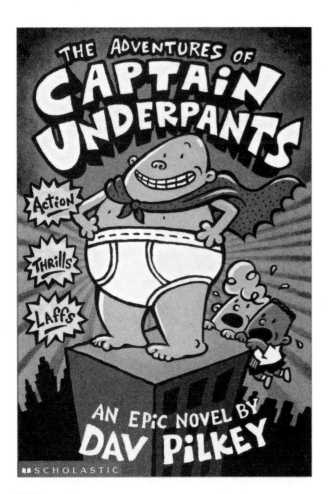

The Adventures
of Captain
Underpants

Dav Pilkey

Scholastic

Schoolboy friends George and Harold are trouble through and through – especially for their headteacher who loathes everything they do, from their endless pranks to their silly giggling. And he particularly hates the Captain Underpants comic they write and produce. But Captain Underpants and his schoolboy inventors are irresistibly entertaining.

How Captain Underpants takes on some important issues of the world and especially all issues to do with underpants is hilariously silly. Told in words and pictures through stories and strip-cartoons, all the adventures unfold at a fast and furious pace, ensuring a feast of entertainment.

'Just perfect for reading in a big dramatic voice with lots of sound effects.'

*Roy Butlin,
Ottakar's Greenwich*

Why share
The Adventures of
Captain Underpants?

☑ Stuffed with enough jokes about underpants to make this a sure-fire winner

☑ A new superhero is born with very special powers

## 5-8 years

### The Worst Witch
Jill Murphy
**Puffin**

Mildred never intends to be the most hopeless new girl at Miss Cackle's Academy for Witches but what do you do when just about everything goes horribly wrong? First there's flying: it's harder than it looks and, on her first trip out, Mildred breaks her broomstick by flying into the yard wall.

Then there's the question of a cat. When it gets to Mildred's turn, all the black cats have gone and Mildred gets a sweet little tabby kitten instead. And then there's the big mistake she makes turning the teacher's pet into a most unusual animal. Nothing seems to go quite right for Mildred but she survives one scrape after another – and gradually learns some magic.

'Reading the stories out loud only does justice to Jill Murphy's colourful characters.'

*Angie Crawford*
*Ottakar's Edinburgh*

## Why share The Worst Witch?

☑ **Funny school story with an additional magical element**

☑ **Mildred Hubble is an endearingly hopeless schoolgirl**

**5-8**
years

**Pippi
Longstocking**
Astrid Lindgren
Illustrated by
Tony Ross
**Oxford**

Pippi Longstocking is nine years old and lives all by herself in Villekulla Cottage with a horse and a pet monkey after her father goes missing on the high seas. But she's never lonely and she can do exactly what she likes! What Pippi likes best is having fun. She's unusually strong, full of high spirits, has a host of crazy ideas and makes up games that no one else has thought of. So, it's not surprising that Tommy and Annika next door love having Pippi round to play, especially as she's always generous and kind. But Pippi can be stubborn too, and doesn't always obey the rules!

Why share Pippi Longstocking?

☑ **Everything is fun when Pippi Longstocking is around**

☑ **Pippi Longstocking's adventures show how much fun playing can be**

## Old Possum's Book of Practical Cats

T. S. Eliot

Illustrated by Nicolas Bentley

**Faber**

Cats of every kind are brilliantly portrayed in T. S. Eliot's classic collection of original and entertaining cat poems. Whatever kind of cat you like, you can find a favourite in this collection. There's Macavity, the Mystery Cat, 'He's the bafflement of Scotland Yard, the Flying Squad's despair:/ For when they reach the scene of crime – Macavity's not there!' Or Gus, the Theatre Cat – a different kind of creature altogether who adores to be centre stage. Or Skimbleshanks, the Railway Cat, whose presence on board the night train is essential if the journey is to go well.

Taken together, the fifteen poems in this collection give a wealth of irrefutable cat lore.

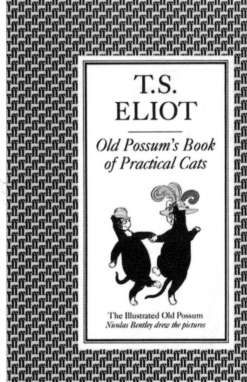

## Why share Old Possum's Book of Practical Cats?

☑ **Witty poems about all kinds of cats**

☑ **Delightful illustrations capture the individual cat characteristics**

## The Hundred-Mile-An-Hour Dog

Jeremy Strong

Illustrated by
Nick Sharratt

**Puffin**

Whoosh! What's that just gone by?

That was Streaker. She's no ordinary dog. Watching her, it's easy to see she's got a touch of Ferrari about her. Not surprisingly, no one in the family is very keen to walk Streaker. But when Trevor is offered £30 to walk her every day of the holidays, he finds it impossible to resist. **MAJOR BRIBERY** does work!

Once landed with the job, Trevor needs to think up a clever plan if he is to survive the holiday . . .

'Produces bursts of laughter and even wins over the cat lovers!'

*Nicola Cowling*
*Librarian, Devon*

## Why share The Hundred-Mile-An-Hour Dog?

☑ **Headlong fun as Trevor tries to keep Streaker under control**

☑ **A brilliant insight into family life**

☑ **Dog-walking will never be the same again!**

## The Velveteen Rabbit

Margery Williams

Adapted by
Lou Fancher

Illustrated by
Steve Johnson and
Lou Fancher

Simon and Schuster

"When a child loves you for a long time, then you become real." That's what the wise old Skin Horse tells the Velveteen Rabbit when he finds himself abandoned in the toy cupboard after Christmas. What the Velveteen Rabbit wants most in the world is to be made 'real' and when his owner can't manage without him, he's sure that it has happened to him. But becoming 'real' comes at a price. Wherever the little boy goes, the Velveteen Rabbit goes too. Gradually his fur gets shabbier, and bit by bit his pink nose gets rubbed away, but it's all worth it in the end.

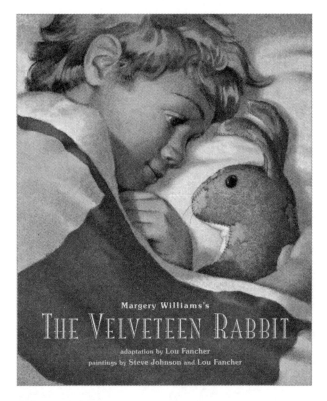

Margery Williams's
## THE VELVETEEN RABBIT

adaptation by Lou Fancher
paintings by Steve Johnson and Lou Fancher

## Why share The Velveteen Rabbit?

☑ **A moving story about believing**

☑ **A touching insight into what toys might feel**

☑ **A classic story of toy magic**

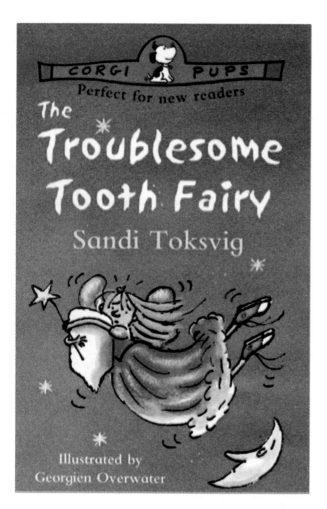

## The Troublesome Tooth Fairy

Sandi Toksvig

Illustrated by
Georgien Overwater

Corgi Pups

When Jessica loses her first tooth, her Granny has a special story to tell her. When she lost her first tooth, she had a rather unusual and almost unfortunate experience. Her tooth was collected by a trainee fairy. It was her very first job and, like all trainees, this fairy didn't really know what she was doing. Skipping through the pages of the manual, she took the child rather than the tooth, shrinking Granny to a suitable fairy-size and then whisking her off to tooth-fairy land. But this magical country built entirely from teeth is no place for real children, and soon both the trainee tooth fairy and Granny are in serious trouble.

Perfectly pitched jokes about a make-believe place with lots of laughs about teeth along the way.

## Why share The Troublesome Tooth Fairy?

☑ **Funny and touching story**

☑ **Warm picture of the relationship between grandparent and grandchild**

## 5-8 years

### Revolting Rhymes

Roald Dahl

Illustrated by
Quentin Blake

**Puffin**

Six familiar stories are made not-so-familiar in Roald Dahl's hilarious, irreverent and sometimes vicious retellings. There's Cinderella, still suffering torment from her Ugly Sisters but now a wiser girl who realizes that the prince may not be such a good bet as a husband. And a new-look Red Riding Hood who's still kind enough to go and visit her Grandmother but also clever enough to carry a pistol tucked into her knickers – just in case. Goldilocks and Snow White are similarly sassy. Breaking and entering is never a nice crime and Goldilocks looks set to come to an unhappy end.

'The only problem is you'll be asked to read it over and over . . .'

*Sarah Drake*
*Ottakar's Science Museum*

## Why share Revolting Rhymes?

- ☑ **Crackling with gruesome humour**

- ☑ **Rollicking verse with witty refrains**

- ☑ **Gives a fresh look on some familiar stories**

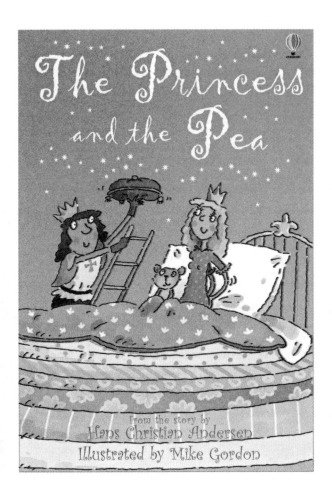

The Princess
and the Pea

Retold by
Susanna Davidson

Illustrated by
Mike Gordon

Usborne

Prince Patrick is sick of all the princesses his father offers him to marry. They are all boring and Patrick can't be sure that they are real. He wants to find his own princess so he sets off to travel the world to find exactly what he wants. And Peg, the kitchen maid, stows away with him. Together they visit a witch who gives Patrick some tips on how to test that a princess is real. A princess must be polite to one and all, kind to rich and poor and have very sensitive skin. Patrick searches high and low visiting Princesses Prudence, Prunella, Primrose and Pavlova. None of them can pass the real princess test. But, luckily, there is someone very near at hand who turns out to be exactly the princess Patrick has been looking for!

## Why share
## The Princess and the Pea?

☑ **A fresh version of a classic story**

☑ **A witty text is matched by amusing illustrations**

## ANDREW MOTION

The book that I've most enjoyed reading aloud to children is *Great Expectations*. Even though some of these children might have been 'too young', the book proves – among other things – how the spell of words can work even when a few of those words might not be understood. The opening pages are enough to prove the point. The mist rolling over the Kent marshes, the gravestones like 'lozenges', the atmosphere of menace and puzzlement – and then the shaggy figure of Magwitch erupting out of nowhere, turning Pip upside down so he sees the church between his flying legs . . . It's all brilliantly

## SIMON MAYO

I will always claim that I read aloud to our three children for their benefit. That it was good for their educational development to sit and listen last thing at night. That somehow, through hearing a story, their creative juices would be stirred. But it was, of course, for me. Nothing could beat the delight of disappearing into a new thrilling chapter. I am certainly no Stephen Fry, but the book is *Harry Potter and the Philosopher's Stone* by J.K. Rowling. What a discovery it was, allowing me to show off my full repertoire of read aloud voices: posh,

## PHILIP PULLMAN

Books that are good to read aloud are not as common as you might think. There's got to be a good story, of course, but there must be something special in the prose – a springiness, an energy, a vividness of rhythm – if it's to be enjoyable for both the reader and the read-to. For my money, few writers approach Robert Louis Stevenson as a supplier of this quality, and few books approach

real and definite, and a wonderful example of symbolic writing as well. After all, it's a book in which normal ideas about 'right' and 'wrong' are often upside down. The criminal Magwitch is kind; the do-gooders are horrible - and so on. Anyway: the book hypnotized me when I was a child, and it's wonderful to see it having the same effect as the years roll by . . .

cockney, camp and Cornish. My camp Cornish delivery is, I believe, unique. Forget the Harry Potter hype, J.K. Rowling created a book that left children desperate for more. And I bet I am not the only parent who, having turned out the light said goodnight to their grateful offspring, sat down on the stairs and read on to find out just how beastly Draco Malfoy could be . . .

*Treasure Island*. But my very favourite book of all to read aloud is Norman Lindsay's rumbustious *The Magic Pudding*, an Australian children's classic of 1918, which has the added benefit of his hilarious drawings to look at and share. It's the funniest children's book ever written. Nothing matches it.

**Enjoy this sample extract from a popular children's classic. This piece gives the sense of the language of the story and also gives the reader a chance to try out some different voices!**

# Clockwork
## or All Wound Up

Once upon a time (when time ran by clockwork), a strange event took place in a little German town. Actually, it was a series of events, all fitting together like the parts of a clock, and although each person saw a different part, no-one saw the whole of it; but here it is, as well as I can tell it.

It began on a winter's evening, when the townsfolk were gathering in the White Horse Tavern. The snow was blowing down from the mountains, and the wind was making the bells shift restlessly in the church tower. The windows were steamed up, the stove was blazing brightly, Putzi the old black cat was snoozing on the hearth; and the air was full of the rich smells of sausage and sauerkraut, of tobacco and beer. Gretl the little barmaid, the landlord's daughter, was hurrying to and fro with foaming mugs and steaming plates.

The door opened, and fat white flakes of snow swirled in, to faint away into water as they met the heat of the parlour. The incomers, Herr Ringelmann the clockmaker and his apprentice Karl, stamped their boots and shook the snow off their greatcoats.

'It's Herr Ringelmann!' said the Burgomaster. 'Well, old friend, come and drink some beer with me! And a mug for young what's his name, your apprentice.'

Karl the apprentice nodded his thanks and went to sit by himself in a corner. His expression was dark and gloomy.

'What's the matter with young thingamajig?' said the Burgomaster. 'He looks as if he's swallowed a thundercloud.'

'Oh, I shouldn't worry,' said the old clockmaker, sitting down at the table with his friends. 'He's anxious about tomorrow. His apprenticeship is coming to an end, you see.'

'Ah, of course!' said the Burgomaster. It was the custom that when a clockmaker's apprentice finished his period of service, he made a new figure for the great clock of Glockenheim. 'So

**Clockwork or
All Wound Up**
Philip Pullman
Illustrated by
Peter Bailey
**Corgi Yearling**

## Clockwork
### or All Wound Up

we're to have a new piece of clockwork in the tower! Well, I look forward to seeing it tomorrow.'

'I remember when my apprenticeship came to an end,' said Herr Ringelmann. 'I couldn't sleep for thinking about what would happen when my figure came out of the clock. Supposing I hadn't counted the cogs properly? Supposing the spring was too stiff? Supposing – oh, a thousand things go through your mind. It's a heavy responsibility.'

THE GREAT CLOCK OF GLOCKENHEIM WAS THE MOST AMAZING PIECE OF MACHINERY IN THE WHOLE OF GERMANY. IF YOU WANTED TO SEE ALL THE FIGURES YOU WOULD HAVE TO WATCH IT FOR A WHOLE YEAR, BECAUSE THE MECHANISM WAS SO COMPLEX THAT IT TOOK TWELVE MONTHS TO COMPLETE ITS MOVEMENT. THERE WERE ALL THE SAINTS, EACH COMING OUT ON THEIR OWN DAY; THERE WAS DEATH, WITH HIS SCYTHE AND HOURGLASS; THERE WERE OVER A HUNDRED FIGURES ALTOGETHER. HERR RINGELMANN WAS IN CHARGE OF IT ALL. THERE NEVER WAS A CLOCK LIKE IT, I PROMISE.

'Maybe so, but I've never seen the lad look so gloomy before,' said someone else. 'And he's not a cheerful fellow at the best of times.'

And it seemed to the other drinkers that Herr Ringelmann himself was a little down-hearted, but he raised his mug with the rest of them and changed the conversation to another topic.

'I hear young Fritz the novelist is going to read us his new story tonight,' he said.

'So I believe,' said the Burgomaster. 'I hope it's not as terrifying as the last one he read to us. D'you know, I woke three times that night and found my hair on end, just thinking about it!'

'I don't know if it's more frightening hearing them here in the parlour, or reading them later on your own,' said someone else.

'It's worse on your own, believe me,' said another. 'You can feel the ghostly fingers creeping up your spine, and even when you know what's going to happen next you can't help jumping when it does.'

Then they argued about whether it was more terrifying to hear a ghost story when you didn't know what was going to happen (because it took you by surprise) or when you did (because there was the suspense of waiting for it). They all enjoyed ghost stories, and Fritz's in particular, for he was a talented storyteller.

'Exciting, scary, romantic and deliciously readable'

*Guardian*

## Charmed Life

Diana Wynne Jones

HarperCollins
Children's Books

When Gwendolen and Cat's parents are drowned in a boating accident, everyone says that it is Gwendolen's powers as a witch that save the siblings. It seems that her gift for magic is exceptional and so the two orphans are swept up to stay at Chrestomanci Castle, home of the greatest wizard of all.

At Chrestomanci Castle, nothing is quite what it seems. And Gwendolen's powers are not what they appear to be either.

With so much magic around, it's no wonder that things do not always go according to plan.

THE ORIGINAL AND THE BEST OF MAGIC

Diana Wynne Jones

CHARMED LIFE

## Why share Charmed Life?

☑ **Awesome magic makes the everyday special but still credible**

☑ **Chrestomanci is an enchanter with exceptional appeal**

☑ *Charmed Life* **opens a door into a whole new world**

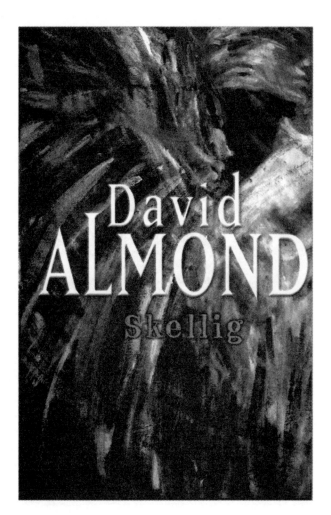

Why share Skellig?

☑ **A rich story that asks serious questions about what is real and what is imaginary**

☑ **A beautifully written story about a child's fears**

**Skellig**
David Almond
**Hodder**

Who is Skellig? That's what Michael needs to find out when he discovers the mysterious creature living in the tumbledown garage at the back of his parent's new home. He appears to be human, asking for a meal from the Chinese takeaway, but he lives half-hidden under spiders' webs and dead flies, and he has wings and he isn't like any human Michael has ever seen before. Is he an angel? Michael needs someone to help him. His baby sister is seriously ill and Michael knows there is a real risk that she'll die. With Mina, the girl who lives nearby, Michael befriends Skellig. They finally bring him out into the light, and Michael's life changes for ever.

'A great story for children who think they are too grown up to be read to.'

*Lesley Sim*
*Librarian, West Sussex*

## Holes

Louis Sachar

**Bloomsbury**

Stanley Yelnats is an unlucky boy. When he is struck by the family curse and falsely accused of stealing a pair of trainers, he is sent off to Camp Green Lake (which is not a camp, not green and not near a lake), a boys' detention centre in the middle of the desert. Every day every boy in the camp has to dig a hole five foot deep and five foot across because, the Warden says, it's good for them.

How can Stanley prove that the Warden has a different and far more sinister motive for wanting so many holes to be dug?

Working as a team with Zero, Armpit and Squid, Stanley outwits the Warden and also breaks his family curse. Above all, he ends the digging of holes!

Ingeniously plotted, Holes is an original and funny story about surviving.

'Unmistakably powerful'
Philip Pullman, *The Guardian*

## Why share Holes?

☑ **A fabulous story of friendship**

☑ **An exceptionally original plot**

'Brilliant reading for anyone with a quirky sense of humour.'

*Debbie Williams*
*Waterstone's*

## Why share Clockwork?

- ☑ **A spooky story that sends shivers down the spine**

- ☑ **Fantastic cast of characters – both real and clockwork**

- ☑ **Gothic storytelling full of surprise and intrigue**

### Clockwork or All Wound Up
Philip Pullman
Illustrated by
Peter Bailey

**Corgi Yearling**

It's a cold winter's night, the snow is falling and several stories begin to collide. There's the story of Karl, the clockmaker's apprentice who is about to fail his first challenge and whose mean spirit and weak temperament bring about his downfall; there's Fritz, whose spine-chilling story unfolds to a critical point but then comes to an abrupt and uneasy end, and there's the sinister presence of Dr Kalmenius, whose unusual power lies at the centre of the whole plot.

A brilliant interweaving of stories of hope and ambition, cowardice and greed, all as delicately balanced as clockwork.

'A stunning, intricately woven tale which suprises from beginning to end.'

*Debbie Williams*
*Waterstone's*

# 8-11 years

## Journey to the River Sea

Eva Ibbotson

**Macmillan**

Orphaned Maia is sent off to stay with her relatives far, far away in the heart of the Amazon jungle. The journey, the thought of life in a strange and different country and the prospect of a new family all fill her with excitement.

Imagine her terrible disappointment when she arrives and finds that her twin cousins, Gwendolyn and Beatrice, are horrid little girls and that her aunt is terrified by everything that lives in the jungle. How will Maia survive?

Luckily, she has been accompanied on her journey by the wonderful governess Miss Minton and together the two of them manage to find the kind of adventures that only somewhere as strange and special as the jungle could reveal.

A charming and magical adventure story that is full of wisdom, warmth and understanding.

'This kind of fun will never fail to delight.' *Philip Pullman*

## Why share Journey to the River Sea?

☑ **A story that brings the Amazon to life for all readers**

☑ **Maia is a feisty heroine who knows what she needs to do to survive**

'Will captivate and enthral listeners at storytime . . . simply beautiful.'

*Emma Swabey, Ottakar's Science Museum*

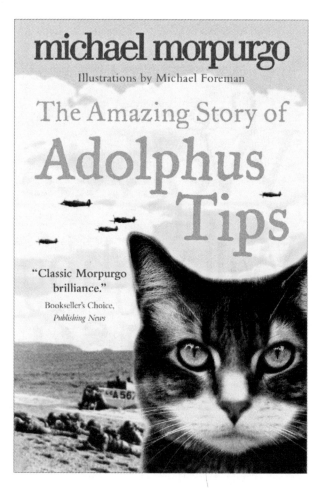

**michael morpurgo**

Illustrations by Michael Foreman

The Amazing Story of
**Adolphus
Tips**

"Classic Morpurgo
brilliance."

Bookseller's Choice,
*Publishing News*

**The Amazing
Story of
Adolphus Tips**
Michael Morpurgo
Illustrated by
Michael Foreman

**HarperCollins
Children's Books**

Adolphus Tips is no
ordinary cat. When the
village of Slapton is
evacuated during the
Second World War,
Adolphus Tips is meant
to leave too. But when
her owner, Lily, and the
rest of her family move
into Uncle George's
farm, Tips is nowhere
to be found.

How will Tips survive
when the village is given
over to training soldiers
as practice for the D-day
landings?

Through the story of one
brave cat, Michael
Morpurgo movingly re-
tells a true story of how
a whole community got
caught up in the war.

## Why share Adolphus Tips?

☑ **Exceptionally poignant story of
how lives are touched by war**

☑ **Written as a diary, each
entry makes a perfect
episode to share**

☑ **A touching account of a
little-known episode of
the Second World War**

## The Wolves of Willoughby Chase

Joan Aiken

**Red Fox**

'You are an orphan, Miss Green, like your cousin, and from now on it is I who have sole say in your affairs. I am your guardian.'

Miss Slighcarp is as chilling as her words sound and she is now in charge of Bonnie and Sylvia. How will they ever escape from her clutches? It would be hard in any circumstances but it is especially hard since the snow lies thick on the ground around Willoughby Chase and the wolves are snapping closer and closer.

Helped on their way by Simon and the flock of geese he is taking to market, Bonnie and Sylvia's journey is a thrilling adventure – and not for the faint-hearted!

'A fabulous story to read on a cold winter's night.'

*Angie Crawford*
*Ottakar's Edinburgh*

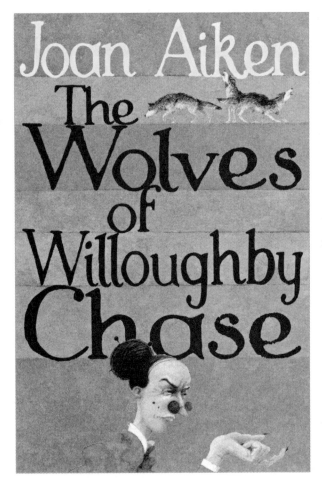

Why share
The Wolves of
Willoughby Chase?

☑ **Fabulous historical fantasy**

☑ **Satisfyingly scary**

☑ **Strong heroines**

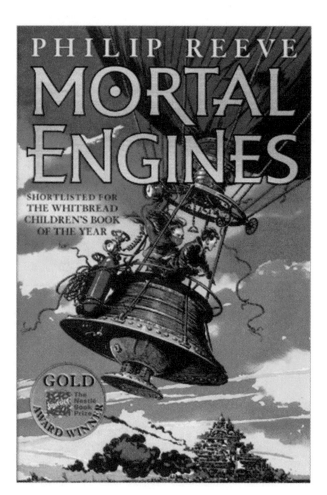

Why share Mortal Engines?

☑ **Thrilling adventure**

☑ **The creation of an exciting new world**

☑ **Brilliant characters**

**Mortal Engines**
Philip Reeve
Scholastic

London is moving: it has been lying low to avoid the other towns which are bigger and more predatory but now it's on the move, chasing a small mining town across the dried-up bed of the old North Sea. Tom is a mere Third Class Apprentice but he is as excited as anyone by the movement of the top-heavy, old city. It's the beginning of a fabulous adventure, especially for Tom and Hester whom he meets after both are pushed out of the speeding City. Tom is desperate to get back on board so that he can unravel the mystery behind what is happening within the many layers of London. But in doing so, he puts his own and Hester's lives in danger. The question is, can he save them both?

'Start reading and you'll be hooked for ever.'

*Debbie Williams*
*Waterstone's*

## Wolf Brother
Michelle Paver
Orion

In the ancient darkness of the forest, in a world steeped in natural magic and primitive terror, Torak must survive. Alone after the death of his father and with a mission to fulfil, he must use all his knowledge and his best instincts to stay alive within the harsh environment of the forest. But he also needs help. Who can Torak trust in a world divided into clans from which he is an outcast? Luckily, Torak finds someone, an orphaned wolf cub, as lost and alone as he is. Together, Torak and his companion, the trusted Wolf Brother, travel to the home of the World Spirit in the High Mountains.

A wonderful quest set in a wholly convincing background and peopled with genuinely brave spirits.

'Simply amazing.'

*Debbie Williams*
*Waterstone's*

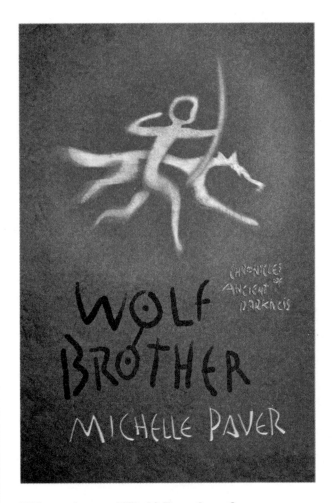

Why share Wolf Brother?

- ☑ **A story of courage and survival**

- ☑ **A thrilling adventure set against a richly described landscape**

- ☑ **An insight into an ancient world and how the people in it lived**

## Why share The Bad Beginning?

☑ **Hilarious dark humour**

☑ **Highly original style**

☑ **Terrific adventure**

'The gloomy narration is hilarious and perfect for reading out loud.'

*Roy Butlin*
*Ottakar's Greenwich*

### The Bad Beginning

Lemony Snicket

Egmont

As its title warns, *The Bad Beginning* is not a happy book. It tells the sorry story of three very unlucky children and the misfortunes that befall them. Like most sad stories, it begins with a terrible accident. The three Baudelaire children are enjoying themselves on the beach when their parents are killed in a terrible fire which destroys everything the family own. Klaus, Violet and baby Sunny must now go and live with Count Olaf, a distant relative whom they have never met.

How they survive life in the filthy house of this disgusting villain who tries to steal their fortune, gives them itchy clothes to wear and feeds them cold porridge makes gloriously depressing reading. A lugubriously funny story for everyone who enjoys disasters and misfortune.

### Harry and the Wrinklies

Alan Temperley

**Scholastic**

When Harry is suddenly orphaned things look as if they are going to get pretty awful. He is dreading being sent off to live with his elderly great-aunts but he soon gets a great shock. They may look old but from the moment he discovers just how fast and furiously they drive, Harry realizes that his aunts are a most unusual pair. When he finds them plotting late into the night it's clear that they are up to no good. He discovers that his aunts' night-time adventures are not exactly regular or legal! That makes them especially good fun for Harry. Now all he has to do is persuade them to let him join in their daring adventures . . .

## Why share Harry and the Wrinklies?

☑ **A gloriously outrageous adventure**

☑ **Larger than life characters**

'Fast-paced narrative and good jokes.'

*Gllian Macdonald, Ottakar's, Edinburgh*

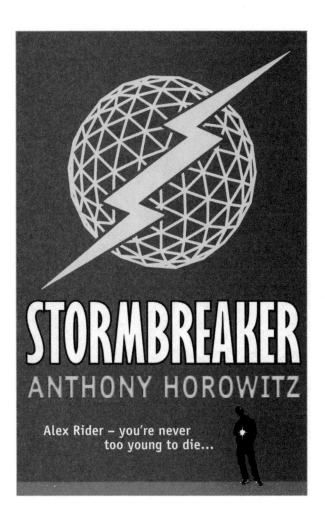

**8-11**
years

**Stormbreaker**
Anthony Horowitz
**Walker Books**

Alex Rider is fourteen when his whole world is turned upside down. Already an orphan, his guardian is killed suddenly and Alex finds himself forcibly recruited into MI6 to train as a superspy. After rigorous training with the SAS, Alex is sent off on his first mission. Even though he's armed with the most up-to-date gadgets available to the service, Alex soon finds himself in danger. Terrible danger. It takes all his courage to survive ... A fabulous story that crackles with suspense and daring and shows that a bit of cheek will take you a very long way.

## Why share Stormbreaker?

- ☑ **Fabulous fantasy of schoolboy who saves the world**

- ☑ **Rip-roaring adventure from start to finish**

'Watch children get closer to the edge of their seats as the tension mounts.'

*Nicola Cowling
Librarian, Devon*

## Measle and the Wrathmonk

Ian Ogilvy

Illustrated by
Chris Mould

**Oxford**

Measle Stubbs is thin
and weedy. And, worse
than that, he hasn't had a
bath for years. And, even
worse than that, he has
to live with his horrible
old guardian, Basil
Tramplebone. In fact,
there's nothing much
that's good about
Measle's life. Little does
he know, however, that
things are about to get
worse. When Measle is
mysteriously zapped into
the world of Basil's toy
train set, everything
takes on a completely
new look. There's
something very nasty
lurking in the rafters and
there's a giant cockroach
on his tail. Measle must
do something – and
quick!

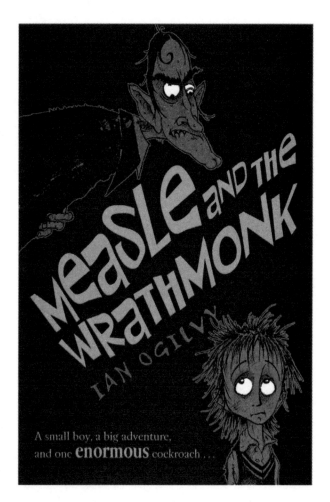

A small boy, a big adventure,
and one **enormous** cockroach . . .

Why share
Measle and the Wrathmonk?

☑ **Rattling adventure of a
brilliantly original kind**

☑ **Measle is a loveable hero
who readers will want
things to go well for**

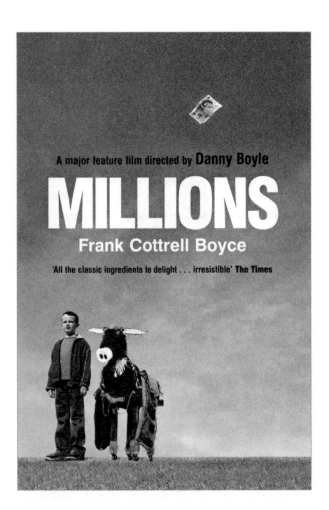

A major feature film directed by **Danny Boyle**

# MILLIONS

## Frank Cottrell Boyce

'All the classic ingredients to delight . . . irresistible' **The Times**

## Millions
### Frank Cottrell Boyce
**Macmillan Children's Books**

When a bag stuffed full of money drops out of a passing train and into their makeshift camp by the railway line, Damian and Anthony suddenly find that they are rich. Very, very rich, to be precise. But there is a problem. They only have a few days in which to spend the money. When the Euro arrives, all their pounds will be worthless.

Damian and Anthony set to work spending with a will. But it's hard to spend without questions being asked and, as they soon discover, money can't buy everything you want. Worse still, there are others out for the money and they are getting frighteningly close.

## Why share Millions?

☑ **A poignant and funny story about money and what it can do**

☑ **A pacy adventure in which the children have to keep ahead of the game**

'A gripping novel which both children and adults will love.'

*Debbie Williams*
*Waterstone's*

## Artemis Fowl
Eoin Colfer
Puffin

Artemis Fowl is only twelve years old but he is already famous as a criminal mastermind. Skilled in the planning and the execution of his crimes, he is used to being able to get what he wants. But when he kidnaps a fairy in his ruthless bid to steal the fairy gold, he finds he has gone a step too far. Captain Holly Short of the LEPrecon unit is more than a match even for Artemis. She's as skilled and dangerous as he is – and she can draw on some extra-special powers to help. And she is not acting alone. Behind her, there's her boss, Commander Root, an elf who'll stop at nothing to get her back. In the headlong adventure that follows, Artemis discovers that fairies are not the creatures that he had been expecting.

'Entertaining and funny, this makes an exciting storytime.'

*Roy Butlin*
*Ottakar's Greenwich*

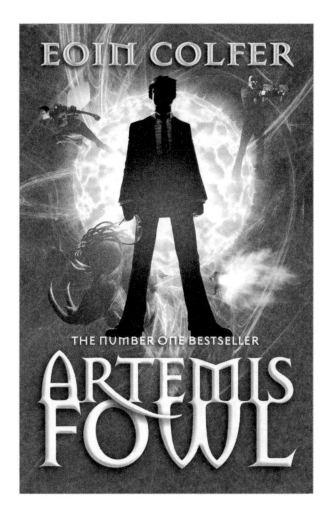

Why share Artemis Fowl?

☑ Fairies, crime and fun – a fabulous adventure

☑ A hi-tech mission with an explosive and original shoot-out

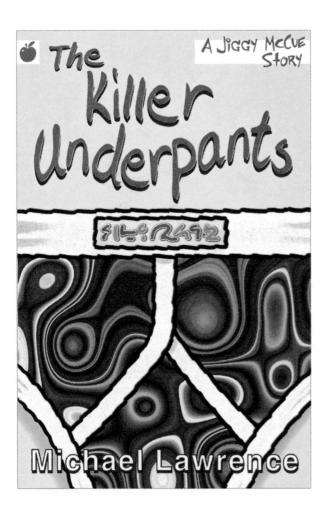

The Killer Underpants

A JIGGY McCUE STORY

Michael Lawrence

## Why share
## The Killer Underpants?

☑ **Good clean fun around a ridiculously silly subject**

'You won't be able to read it without bursting into giggles.'

*Angie Crawford*
*Ottakar's, Edinburgh*

**8-11** years

**The Killer Underpants**
Michael Lawrence
Orchard Books

When Jiggy's mum gets an idea into her head, there's no stopping her. This time, she's absolutely sure that Jiggy needs a new pair of underpants. His old ones are just too holey even though, as Jiggy points out, holes are good in underpants. Jiggy uses his best powers of persuasion to stop her but to no avail. New underpants it is! But even Jiggy couldn't have known just how much trouble these underpants would cause. They are evil. They make Jiggy scratch, they make Jiggy itch, and whatever Jiggy says under the influence of the underpants happens. When Jiggy finds out that the man who sold them to his mum is Neville the Devil whose motto is Mischief is My Business, he knows he'll have to think up something very special indeed to free himself from the terrible underpants.

## The Giggler Treatment

Roddy Doyle

Scholastic

When Mister Mack steps out to catch the train to his work in the biscuit factory one morning, little does he know that he is about to step into a huge pile of stinking dog poo. Why is he about to step in the dog poo? Because the Gigglers have put it there to pay Mister Mack back for what he did last night. Who are the Gigglers? The Gigglers protect children from adults who are unkind. But, for once, they've made a mistake. Mister Mack was only unkind for a moment and the dog-poo treatment is not necessary. Can the Gigglers, helped by **Rover** who supplied the poo, stop Mister Mack before his foot makes the squelchy, squishy contact?

A hectic adventure prevents a nasty accident!

'Silly and funny and all about poo! What could be better?'

*Roy Butlin*
*Ottakar's Greenwich*

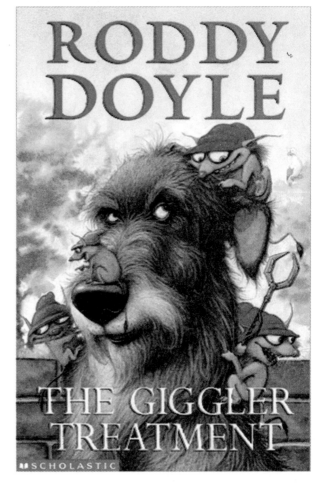

## Why share The Giggler Treatment?

☑ **Hilarious fun of a (nearly) disgusting nature**

☑ **Every child needs to know about the Gigglers!**

**Awful End**
Philip Ardagh
Faber

When Eddie Dickens' parents are struck down by a strange disease that turns them a rather peculiar shade of yellow and makes them smell like old hot water bottles, Eddie is sent to live at Awful End. He's worried that things will not go well. And he's right. After all, his Mad Uncle Jack, the thinnest of thin beaky-nosed gentlemen, and his Even Madder Aunt Maud who has a stuffed stoat called Malcolm, live at Awful End and, with them around, no one could have very high hopes of how things could turn out. The things that happen at Awful End are extremely daft, extremely smelly and extremely good fun.

Why share Awful End?

- ☑ Ludicrous fun in a smelly environment

- ☑ Enjoy a host of unusual characters – and grow to love them

## Cloud Busting

Malorie Blackman

**Corgi**

Davey is the new boy and he is odd. Everyone thinks so, but it is Sam who leads the way, giving Davey the nickname 'Fizzy Feet' and finding every way possible of making fun of him. But it's worse than that. When Sam and Davey are alone, they are firm friends and Sam knows that Davey is odd, yes, and different, but also special. He even knows something secret about Davey – and promises never to tell. But Sam can't resist. Surely it won't matter?

Written as a series of poems using different forms including limerick, haiku and blank verse, *Cloud Busting* is a hugely thoughtful insight that penetrates right to the heart of the issue: how do I be true to myself?

Why share Cloud Busting?

- ☑ **Celebration of the importance of friendship**

- ☑ **A wise exploration of peer pressures**

- ☑ **Different poetic forms give original and special impact**

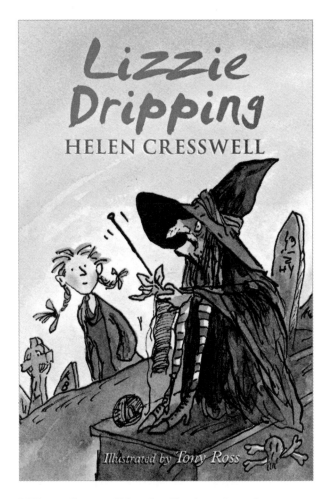

**Lizzie Dripping**
Helen Cresswell
Oxford

Lizzie Dripping is a dreamy girl who has a habit of not doing anything quite right. It is not surprising really, as she is always off on an adventure inside her own head which makes her forget what she is meant to be doing.

There's the time that Lizzie 'forgets' that she is being all grown up and looking after her baby brother, and sets off blackberry picking instead . . .

And then there's the witch whom Lizzie finds sitting in the graveyard busy doing her knitting. Of course, no one believes Lizzie. After all, why would there be a witch in the graveyard and why can only Lizzie see her?

Five delightful stories about Lizzie, a little girl with a very special gift for causing mayhem around her!

## Why share Lizzie Dripping?

☑ **A strong-minded girl who has great adventures**

☑ **Anyone who knows what it feels like to be in the wrong will love Lizzie Dripping**

☑ **Perfectly created blend of the magical and the everyday**

## 8-11 years

### Ruby Holler

Sharon Creech

Bloomsbury

Yes. Love can change people. It's true! That's what Dallas and Florida find when they are asked to go and live with Tiller and Sairy Morley.

Dallas and Florida have lived all of their lives in Boxton Creek Home. And that's where they expect to stay as no one else ever seems to want them for long.

But the Morleys do want them to stay and make a new life in Ruby Holler. The Morleys are different. They play games with Dallas and Florida and they lead them on some wild adventures. They know that in Ruby Holler Dallas and Florida may become different children. And, slowly but surely, they do.

'Sensitively written, this book tackles issues of family learning, loyalty and belonging.'

*Grace Print*
*Ottakar's Bromley*

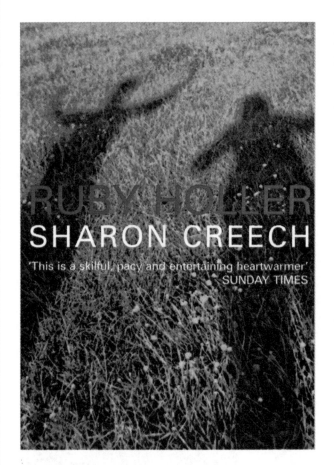

Why share Ruby Holler?

☑ **A moving story about healing through love**

☑ **Wonderfully written and full of insight into how pain can be soothed**

☑ **A story of hope and trust – and cookies!**

'A powerful, absorbing and unusual novel' *The Bookseller*

## Why share Witch Child?

☑ **A deeply moving story of one child's courage in the face of adversity**

☑ **A brilliant picture of life under the Puritans**

### Witch Child
Celia Rees
**Bloomsbury**

Mary's diary of 1659 tells the story of her life from the moment when she first finds herself in grave danger after the arrest, imprisonment, 'trial' and finally hanging of her grandmother for witchcraft. These are troubled times but Mary is helped to escape to safety and set on the road to a new life and a new identity over the sea in America. But there's prejudice there too, and Mary has to keep her wits about her and her skills hidden to survive the mistrust that is rife amongst the new settlers. Mary's insight into the true motives of many of the so-called 'good' people is shocking but convincing while the courage she shows as she weaves her way through their corruption and false values is inspiring.

'Listeners will be captivated by this beautifully written story.'

*Jonathon Lloyd*
*Ottakar's Greenwich*

125

## The More the Merrier

Anne Fine
Doubleday

Love it or loathe it, Christmas is a time for families to get together. The plan is for them to have fun but, in Ralph's house at least, that is easier said than done! There's Uncle Tristram whose idea of a good time is to throw the spuds at the cat, Great-Aunt Ida who's lost most of the plot already, the twins Sylvester and Sylvia, and worst of all from Ralph's point of view at least, Cousin Titania. Can Ralph (and indeed his mother) survive the festive season?

## Why share The More the Merrier?

☑ **A witty look at the fun and not-so-much-fun moments of Christmas**

☑ **Anne Fine's sharp eye captures all the best and worst moments of family life**

# Index

# ACKNOWLEDGEMENTS

With grateful thanks to:

Jacqueline Wilson, Nick Sharratt, Julia Eccleshare,
David Higham Associates, Colman Getty PR

Kelly Cauldwell, Ian Lansley,
Naomi Cooper, Alison Gadsby

Malorie Blackman, Cherie Booth QC,
Anne Fine, Shelia Hancock, Charlie Higson,
Ruth Kelly MP, Michael Morpurgo,
Andrew Motion, Michael Palin, Philip Pullman,
J.K. Rowling, Imogen Stubbs,
Eleanor Updale, Terry Wogan

Andersen Press, Bloomsbury, Child's Play,
Egmont, Faber, HarperCollins Childrens Books,
Hodder Children's Books, Macmillan Children's Books,
Orchard Books, Orion, Oxford University Press,
Puffin, Scholastic Children's Books,
Simon and Schuster, Usborne, Walker Books

Borders, Ottakar's, Waterstone's, WHSmith,
Peters Library Services, Scholastic Clubs and Fairs